THE Graduate School of Education, Harvard University, is actively interested in the publication of material which will help to interpret various selected phases of educational theory and practice. The volumes already published have, for the most part, been written by members of the Harvard faculty and by advanced students working directly with instructors in the Graduate School of Education. The Committee on Publications will, however, consider manuscripts from educators who have carried on their investigations elsewhere, provided the material be of unusual worth and distinction.

The titles appearing in the advertising pages of this book indicate the general scope of our work. The list will be constantly augmented by material of value to teachers, administrators, and the public.

The School will gladly answer questions on any of these books and pamphlets. Such inquiries may be addressed to *The Committee on Publications, Graduate School of Education, Lawrence Hall, Harvard University, Cambridge 38, Massachusetts.*

HARVARD STUDIES IN EDUCATION

[Volumes not listed are out of print.]

5. *The Intelligence of Continuation School Children in Massachusetts.* By L. Thomas Hopkins $1.75
6. *The Financial Support of State Universities.* By R. R. Price $3.50
7. *Individual Differences in the Intelligence of School Children.* By Mary M. Wentworth $2.00
8. *The Vocational Guidance of College Students.* By Lewis Adams Maverick $2.50
9. *The Small Junior High School.* By Francis T. Spaulding . . $2.50
11. *Individual Instruction in English Composition.* By Stephen DeWitt Stephens $2.50
12. *An Approach to Composition through Psychology.* By Phyllis Robbins $3.00
13. *Counseling the College Student.* By Helen D. Bragdon . . $2.50
14. *Education and International Relations.* By Daniel Alfred Prescott $2.50
15. *Educational Achievement in Relation to Intelligence.* By Charles W. St. John $3.50
16. *The Educational Work of Thomas Jefferson.* By Roy J. Honeywell $3.00
17. *Examining the Examination in English.* By Charles Swain Thomas and others $2.00
18. *Achievement in the Junior High School.* By Bancroft Beatley $2.00
20. *The Sound Motion Picture in Science Teaching.* By Phillip Justin Rulon $2.50
21. *The Fusion of Social Studies in Junior High Schools.* By H. E. Wilson. 1933. . . . . $2.50
22. *The School and the Community: A Study of Local Control in the Public Schools of Massachusetts.* By L. Leland Dudley $2.50
24. *An Historical Study of Examinations and Grading Systems in Early American Universities.* By Mary Lovett Smallwood . $2.00
25. *A Tercentenary History of Boston Public Latin School, 1635–1935.* By Pauline Holmes $3.50
27. *Incentives to Composition: An Approach to Writing through Subject Stimulus.* By Phyllis Robbins $2.75
28. *An Experimental Comparison of Two Shorthand Systems.* By Walter L. Deemer and Phillip J. Rulon $3.00
29. *The Influence of the Enlightenment on the Catholic Theory of Religious Education in France, 1750–1850.* By Clarence Edward Elwell $3.50

HARVARD UNIVERSITY PRESS
CAMBRIDGE, MASSACHUSETTS

HARVARD STUDIES IN EDUCATION
PUBLISHED UNDER THE DIRECTION OF
THE GRADUATE SCHOOL OF EDUCATION

VOLUME 30

LONDON : GEOFFREY CUMBERLEGE
OXFORD UNIVERSITY PRESS

AMERICAN REGIONALISM
and
SOCIAL EDUCATION

A STUDY OF THE IMPLICATIONS OF AMERICAN REGIONALISM
FOR THE SOCIAL-STUDIES PROGRAMS IN NEW ENGLAND SCHOOLS

BY

ROYCE H. KNAPP

ASSOCIATE PROFESSOR OF SECONDARY EDUCATION
UNIVERSITY OF NEBRASKA

HARVARD UNIVERSITY PRESS
CAMBRIDGE
1947

COPYRIGHT, 1947
BY THE PRESIDENT AND FELLOWS OF HARVARD COLLEGE

PRINTED AT THE HARVARD UNIVERSITY PRINTING OFFICE
CAMBRIDGE, MASSACHUSETTS, U. S. A.

ACKNOWLEDGMENTS

DURING THE PREPARATION of this study I have enjoyed the help and counsel of many people. Teachers and supervisors in many New England schools coöperated in the survey of the teaching of the social studies. Leaders and specialists who patiently granted personal interviews and answered written queries were a valuable source of information, and I am very much in their debt. Personnel of the New England Council and the New England Regional Planning Commission gave freely of their time and helped in the collection of much primary source material. For countless hours of encouragement I am indebted to Professors Henry Wyman Holmes, Robert Ulich, Alfred D. Simpson, and William H. Burton of the Faculty of Education at Harvard. For constructive criticism I am indebted to Mr. Tyler Kepner of the Brookline, Massachusetts Public Schools; Mr. Richard J. Stanley, West Hartford, Connecticut Public Schools; Mr. Roland B. Greeley of the New England Regional Planning Commission; and Professors Earl E. Lackey and Frank E. Sorenson of the University of Nebraska. For personal guidance since the inception of the study I am particularly grateful to Dr. Howard E. Wilson, formerly of the Faculty of Education at Harvard, now of the Carnegie Endowment for International Peace.

ROYCE H. KNAPP

December 16, 1946

CONTENTS

I. THE SETTING, PROBLEM, AND PROCEDURE OF THE STUDY 3
   The Philosophical Setting, 3
   American Regionalism and Social Education, 5
   The Problem of This Study, 9
   Method and Sources, 10

II. AMERICAN REGIONALISM AND THE SOCIAL SCIENCES 13
   Geography and Regionalism, 14
   Economics and Regionalism, 20
   Political Science and Regionalism, 24
   Anthropology and Regionalism, 28
   Sociology and Regionalism, 30
   Literary and Aesthetic Regionalism, 33
   Summary, 36
   American Regionalism and the Social Studies, 37

III. NEW ENGLAND AS AN AMERICAN REGION . . . 41
   Setting and Resources, 42
   Population and Cultural Heritage, 48
   Economy, 51
   Some Important Regional Problems, 59
   Recent Trends in Regional Integration and Coöperation, 66
   Summary, 71

IV. THE STUDY OF NEW ENGLAND REGIONAL LIFE IN NEW ENGLAND SCHOOLS 73
   The Opinions of State Supervisors, 73
   The Opinions of Social-Studies Leaders, 75
   An Analysis of Widely Used Social-Studies Textbooks, 76
   What the Teachers Say, 84
   Conclusions, 90

V. WHAT NEW ENGLAND SCHOOLS OUGHT TO TEACH
ABOUT NEW ENGLAND REGIONAL LIFE 93

Area I. The Regional Resources of New England, 93
Area II. The Regional Population, 95
Area III. The History of New England, 96
Area IV. The Regional Economy of New England, 98
Area V. The Governments of New England, 99
Area VI. The Regional Culture of New England, 100
Area VII. The Regional Problems of New England, 102
Summary, 103

VI. PLANS AND MATERIALS FOR ADJUSTING THE SOCIAL-
STUDIES PROGRAMS OF NEW ENGLAND SCHOOLS
TO THE LIFE AND PROBLEMS OF NEW ENGLAND 104

Introducing the Seven Areas of Content on New England,
104: Elementary Schools, 104; Junior High Schools, 106;
Senior High Schools, 108
The Problem of Materials, 115: Available Resources, 115;
Materials Needed, 116
Recommendations for Teacher Training, 120
Recommendations for Regional Coöperation, 121
American Regionalism and National Welfare, 122

APPENDICES 125

A. Letter of Inquiry Sent to New England State Supervisors
and Social-Studies Leaders, 127
B. State Department Supervisors Who Participated in the
Social-Studies Survey, 128
C. Social-Studies Leaders and Curriculum Specialists, 129
D. Social-Studies Textbooks Widely Used in New England
Schools, 130
E. Resources and Teaching Aids for Teaching the Life and
Problems of New England, 135

BIBLIOGRAPHY 141

INDEX 155

MAPS

FIGURE
1. Physical Divisions of the United States 17
2. Climates of the United States 18
3. Major Soil Divisions of the United States 18
4. Vegetation Regions of the United States 19
5. Major Geographic Regions of the United States 19
6. Manufactural Regions of the United States 23
7. Agriculture Regions of the United States 23
8. Regionalism in Politics 25
9. Land Use Problem Regions 27
10. Culture Areas of the North American Indian 29
11. Metropolitan Regions in the United States 32
12. Regions of Socio-Economic Homogeneity 32
13. New England in the United States 42
14. New England: Physiographic Regions 44
15. New England: Types of Farming 56

AMERICAN REGIONALISM AND SOCIAL EDUCATION

CHAPTER I
THE SETTING, PROBLEM, AND PROCEDURE OF THE STUDY

If we forget the dependence of education upon its environment, we are likely to cherish mistaken opinions of what the school can contribute to the future of the nation. — Robert Ulich

The Philosophical Setting

THE FUNDAMENTAL TENETS which underly this study and influence its approach, its method, and its recommendations should be stated at the outset. The following paragraphs present a statement and a brief elaboration of these tenets, the philosophical foundations of the work.

1. *If schools are to prepare young people for competent adulthood in society, they must always operate within the economic, social, political, and moral ideals and values of society.* Schools are institutions created and supported by society for training youth in social competence. They are expected to foster the continuous welfare of society, and this means the fostering of its dominant values and ideals. To prepare youth for life in the society which supports schools, the schools must be in harmony with the commonly held social philosophy as expressed in current views of the social economy, the social welfare, the social controls and laws, and the principal moral tenets of society.

2. *A fundamental part of the preparation of youth for social competence consists in giving youth the best possible understanding of society.* Of course young people receive education from other social institutions and from the daily contacts of life, but schools have the responsibility for presenting systematic and critical understandings of society in a relatively objective

manner. To accomplish this objective the schools must present youth with the historical development, the geographical foundation, the economy, the social values, and the social controls of society. Competence is usually based upon experience and knowledge. It is the duty of the schools to present the most pertinent social knowledge to young people, and, as far as possible, to give them experiences which will lead to social competence.

3. *In most American schools the social studies carry the major responsibility for presenting the best possible understandings of society to youth.* The social studies consist primarily of segments of history, government, geography, economics, sociology, psychology, and philosophy, selected in the light of educational purposes and adapted to the age and ability of youth. The content of the social studies in American schools deals largely with human group living. These studies attempt to describe and to interpret society to youth. Not only do the social studies deal with the whole society, but they deal also with the present lives of the young people themselves and with their observations of the life around them.

4. *Since society is in many respects in constant flux, and since new descriptions, interpretations, and analyses are continually being produced, the social-studies programs of the schools must reflect these newer findings if they are to function effectively in bringing youth to socially competent adulthood.* Social research is not static. New research is constantly shedding a finer light upon our society. Only by incorporating the results of significant social research can the social-studies programs be made to accomplish their purpose for youth.

5. *There is continuous need for educators to analyze developments in the social sciences to the end that recent and vital findings are included within the social-studies programs of the schools.* Such study by competent educators who are trained in the social sciences will give education a firmer foundation. It will produce a closer integration of contemporary American

life and the curriculum of the school. It will gear the school to the economic and political realities of modern society. One educator, surveying the American educational system, has concluded, "Our education has been afraid of realities." [1] If educators had been constantly aware of the evolution of society and the growth of its problems and complexities, and if they had made the proper curricular adjustments, this charge could not be made.

AMERICAN REGIONALISM AND SOCIAL EDUCATION

Recent decades have witnessed the rapid rise and development of a promising method and philosophy of research in the several social sciences which places emphasis upon organic areas of human group living so that human life is visualized and studied against the backdrop of environment. This method and philosophy is called regionalism. The regional approach emphasizes cultural phenomena which cannot be measured exactly, such as folkways, the spirit of peoples, the folklore, and personality. These phenomena are part of the American scene, but as yet they have not received proper study and interpretation in American schools. It is time some consideration of them became part of the subject matter of the schools which hope to interpret this country to youth. Regionalism entails a study and an appreciation of the diversity of American culture, but it entails also an appreciation of the idea that this diversity is a part of a total scene. The totality is rich because its parts are rich and varied. This is the theme of regionalism.

The social scientists who take the regional approach to the study of America envisage a further step: the regeneration of the nation and the reordering of the total scene in terms of its parts. This movement is called regional planning. Planning on a regional basis means that the attack on social problems will take place at the regional level in terms of the regional en-

[1] Henry Wyman Holmes, *The Road to Courage* (New York: Alfred A. Knopf, Inc., 1943).

vironment and people. It means planning for areas smaller than the nation and larger than the local communities and states.

Beyond these meanings of regionalism are the meanings which grow out of regional administration of government, the regional organization of large industries and businesses, and the literary and aesthetic regionalism of writers and artists. Whereas the accent in American life was once on the nation as a whole or upon individual localities and states, the accent now seems to be upon regions consisting of groups of states.

The implications of regionalism for education have been the subject of considerable study and much research and writing by educators. A. C. Krey produced one of the first of these studies at the University of Minnesota.[2] With the assistance and collaboration of several students and teachers in the field, Krey attempted to build a program of social studies for an agricultural region which specialized in dairying and the production of small grains. The educator who studies Krey's work finds some confusion, however. The curriculum listed is practically the same as any typical curriculum of social studies. The program presented is not a great departure from what literally thousands of schools have been doing. Certainly it is not in the best sense a regional program for the social studies. It is merely a program for the social studies which tells teachers to draw attention to the "community," the "local region," and sometimes, "local regions." There is confusion of terms throughout the study, and it is never certain what Krey means by a region. There is no evidence to show that the curriculum ought to teach specific ideas about the region. Only vague references are given, like "Noting developments in grain and dairy industries," in grades five and six, or "Locating same and similar activities — vocations and avocations — in local community."[3] Nowhere

[2] *A Regional Program for the Social Studies* (New York: The Macmillan Company, 1938).
[3] A. C. Krey, *op. cit.*, p. 58.

is there a discussion of the factors which make a region a region, and nowhere is there a discussion of what the problems of the region are or the problems of youth in the region.

The Progressive Education Association has sponsored a study of regional planning and its relation to education for the purpose of discovering the research studies available and bringing them together for use by teachers and administrators. Under the chairmanship of Professor Paul R. Hanna, of Stanford University, a preliminary report was mimeographed and distributed in 1939.[4] This report called attention to the reasons why we are compelled to think in terms of regions, the role of education in utilizing the resources of a region for optimum well-being, the way in which regions are determined, and the major regions of the United States. Perhaps the finest contribution of the report was its excellent bibliography on each of the major American regions. The report has been a valuable aid in this study, and it has served as a useful tool in education workshops throughout the nation. The report envisioned the time when schools and colleges would function as organs of "social sensitivity and as a laboratory to which the citizens of the region would bring common problems for study and solution."[5] Regional development would be the final objective of such education.

Aubrey Hahn studied community schools in the Pacific Northwest to determine their role in educating for the use of the natural and human resources in the region.[6] He outlined existing programs which attempt to educate youth with respect to conservation of the resources of nature, and the evidence of such problems in the local community. Hahn held that the local community school has the responsibility of acquainting youth

---

[4] *The Role of Education in Utilizing Regional Resources: A Preliminary Report* (New York: Progressive Education Association, 1939).
[5] *The Role of Education in Utilizing Regional Resources: A Preliminary Report* (Progressive Education Association, 1939), p. 2: 10.
[6] "The Role of the Community School in Educating for the Use of the Natural and Human Resources of the Pacific Northwest Region," unpublished doctoral dissertation, Stanford University, 1940.

with regional problems, with conservation ideals and activities, and with the meaning of regional well-being.

Ellis F. Hartford has produced a voluminous doctoral dissertation which deals with the regional resources and problems of the Southeast and their implications for the formulation of educational policy in the region.[7] Hartford insisted that it was one of the principal responsibilities of education to deal with the problems of the region, not only for the enrichment of the educational pattern itself, but for the creation of a regenerated regional life. He believed that the schools can teach the facts about the region for intelligent choice among the alternatives which a region could choose for future development. Moreover, he believed that it was one of the functions of education to help synthesize the findings of the regional scholars and the government and private agencies interested in the development of a region. The formulation of educational policy, Hartford believed, ought to be based upon the needs of the region in which education is to take place.

The studies mentioned, and the articles dealing with the regionalism and education in periodical literature, which are too numerous to describe, form the principal literature and thought on the role of education in regional planning and development. Many regionalists have dealt with the implications of education for regional balance, and many leaders in education have called for adjustment of the program of education for American youth to the life and problems of the home region. Among those who have emphasized these ideas in articles and speeches are Professor George T. Renner of Columbia University, Professor Howard E. Wilson of Harvard University, Professor Howard W. Odum of the University of North Carolina, Professor Lewis Mumford of Stanford University, and Professor Paul R. Hanna of Stanford University. Each has written articles and given addresses on various aspects of regionalism and education.

The present treatment grew out of a study of the work of

[7] "Educational Policy for Regional Well-Being with Reference to the Southeast," unpublished doctoral dissertation, Harvard University, 1942.

SETTING, PROBLEM, AND PROCEDURE

these various regionalists and educators in the attempt to formulate a program of social studies for the New England region. The writer's efforts along this line began in a workshop course in the social studies at the Graduate School of Education, Harvard University, during 1940 and 1941. At that time the writer coöperated with a group of teachers from New England schools in building a test on the life and character of New England for secondary schools. These recent studies and some minor research project [8] underly the present study of regionalism in American life and scholarship and its implications for a program of social studies in New England.

THE PROBLEM OF THIS STUDY

The problem of the present study grows out of the philosophy set forth in the foregoing paragraphs and out of the recent developments of regionalism in American life and American scholarship. It grows out of the compelling common problems of an old American region — New England. The writer believes that it is a major responsibility of the social-studies program of New England schools to help in the realization of a stable future for the people of New England. Furthermore, he believes that the scholarship and aspirations of the regionalists have special implications for the social-studies programs in New England schools in terms of content and objectives and materials. The realities of New England life and the scholars of regionalism combine to thrust aside the recent generalizations of cynics and pessimists who insist that New England is "going to seed," has reached its "Indian Summer," or "lacks its great colonial spirit." New England has excellent potentialities in its human and natural resources, and, although the region has been passing through a long period of depression and crisis, it now has at hand the assets with which to build a finer future.

The problem of this study can be stated as an attempt to

[8] Royce H. Knapp, *A Bibliography of the New England Region, and a List of Unit Titles* (Mimeographed; Cambridge: Harvard Graduate School of Education, 1941); "American Regionalism and Social Education," *Social Education*, December 1942, pp. 362–365.

adjust the social-studies programs of New England schools to the life and problems of New England. The different steps in the solving of this problem are (1) analyzing the works of American regionalists to discover the meanings of regionalism in the social sciences and in American life, in order to indicate the implications of regionalism for the social studies in American schools; (2) surveying and analyzing the works which have dealt with New England as an American region, in order to write a summary analysis of the life and problems of New England; (3) surveying the social-studies programs in New England schools, in order to determine to what extent New England schools are now informing youth about the economy, resources, problems, and recent social trends of New England; (4) formulating a statement of what the social-studies programs of New England schools ought to teach New England youth about the life and problems of New England; and (5) presenting plans for implementing the suggested program for the social studies, and a discussion of the materials available for teaching the regional life of New England, together with a statement of needed materials for educational purposes.

Method and Sources

The method of the study grows out of the different parts of its problem, and each part will form a section in this discussion.

(1) The works of the American regionalists are the source of statements on the meaning of regionalism in American life and in American scholarship. The implications for the social studies will be developed from the philosophy underlying the present study, which has already been stated.

(2) The works of scholarship in the fields of history, geography, economics, government, sociology, and literature which have dealt with New England are the source of a summary analysis of the life and problems of New England.

(3) The survey of the social-studies programs of New England schools will take several forms. A questionnaire was sent

to teachers of the social studies, listing topics on the various facets of New England life and problems, in order to determine what the schools are teaching. The textbooks most widely used in the social-studies programs of New England schools form another source and clue to the content of the social-studies programs of New England schools. A selected list of supervisors of social studies and of leaders throughout the region who have wide knowledge of the curriculum of social studies in New England, and two members of each state department of education in New England have been queried concerning the content of social studies and the teaching of New England life to New England youth. The writer is familiar with the social-studies programs of many New England schools through having taught temporarily in one Boston metropolitan school and through personal acquaintanceship with several supervisors throughout the region.

(4) The recommendations for adjusting the social-studies programs of New England schools to the life and problems of the region will be developed from a discussion of the needs of New England, the needs of youth in New England, and the present program of teaching the regional life of New England.

(5) The writer has made a considerable study of the resources which are available for educating youth with respect to the life and problems of New England, and therefore can present a summary of available materials. Materials will be suggested to aid teachers and administrators in the program of social studies suggested for acquainting New England youth with the life and problems of New England.

A note should be added here with respect to the method of this study. It is granted that the approach to the problem is somewhat subjective and intuitive, and that it arises in no small part from the observations and experiences of the writer. It is believed that it would be difficult to approach this problem in a manner which would carry statistical accuracy and scientific proof of all observations and conclusions. The problems of the social studies are human problems, and they are not all susceptible to the accuracy of physics, chemistry, or mathematics. Most of the great problems of the social studies have been resolved through the use of the best evidence available and the consideration of the great values of society and the needs of men, to the end that the best choice of one man or a group of men could be made. The acceptance of a philosophy for the purposes of the social studies and the use of that philosophy in research and teaching are often the result of intuitive and subjective judgments.

CHAPTER II

AMERICAN REGIONALISM AND THE SOCIAL SCIENCES

THE REGIONAL IDEA is present in the ordinary day-to-day conversations of most people. Humanity in general, when speaking of remote or foreign areas, commonly uses such terms as the Balkans, the Far East, the Middle East, the South, the Middle West, New England. It is the accepted method of designating and talking about the various areas of the earth. Sometimes the accent is on a political region; sometimes the geographical features are emphasized, and sometimes others among the various facets of a regional environment or life. But in all these senses the denominator "region" designates a culture in a place. People are labeled according to their place of origin: a person from Alabama is called a Southerner, a person from New Hampshire, a New Englander, and a person from Idaho, a Westerner. These are some common uses of the regional idea in many conversations in which nearly everybody participates.

Scholars in the social sciences have taken part of their philosophy from the commonly held assumptions of mankind, and it is believed that their approach to regionalism is partially the result simply of looking at society. But the scholarly descriptions, interpretations, and analyses of society which take the regional approach must necessarily be more objective than the ordinary discussions of mankind. The regionalists of the social sciences must use the best data available to reach their conclusions and their conceptions of what society is like. For several decades their studies of society have increasingly given importance to the regional approach, and there now exists an abundant literature on regionalism as a method of interpreting social life, and as a method of scientific research in the social sciences.

The purpose in this chapter is to discuss the meaning of regionalism in the several social sciences, and to present some of the research of social scientists which shows the regional nature of American life.

The topics for discussion will evolve about each of the several social sciences. In each instance the concept of regionalism held in each social science will be presented. It is noteworthy that there exist many meanings of regionalism, and a wide diversity of opinion on what a region is. In some instances it will seem that there is overlapping in the various fields of the social sciences, but it will be noted that in each field the regionalists choose their regional techniques to fit their separate and individual purposes. Thus it is necessary to review each of the social sciences for concepts of regionalism in order to find their common approaches to the regional concept. After presenting the study of the meaning of regionalism in American life the implications for social-studies programs can be stated in terms of the philosophy of the thesis which was stated in Chapter I.

Geography and Regionalism

Perhaps the regional method of study first came to maturity in the field of geography. Though geographers have for centuries dealt largely with the physical factors of the earth, modern scholars in this field take the human factor into account as an important feature of the environment. The change in emphasis was first manifested in Germany, France, and England during the nineteenth century, when men like Ritter, Brunhes, Ratzel, Herbertson, and Unstead began to give emphasis to the role of man in effecting changes in and using the natural environment.[1] During the nineteenth century two schools of thought evolved in geography, and to some extent the

---

[1] R. E. Dickinson and O. J. R. Howarth, *The Making of Geography* (Oxford: Clarendon Press, 1933), p. 208.

two are still present. One school believed that the environment of nature was the principal determinant of the activities of mankind, and it placed strict and inexorable limitations upon what men could accomplish. This school has been called the environmentalist or determinist school. The most important leaders were Friedrich Ratzel, a German, and his American disciple, Ellen Churchill Semple. Naturally their studies and the studies of their followers emphasized the use of natural regions — determined by climate, soils, topography, geologic structures — as types of regions for studies of geography. Opposed to this school of geography were the "possibilists," or human geographers who believed that man was the most significant factor in determining how mankind would live and in the use of the land. They believed that everywhere the earth presented potentialities, and that man could apply his intelligence to selecting regions for occupation and utilization for human purposes. The leaders of this school were P. Vidal de la Blache, Jean Brunhes, and J. Russell Smith. Their studies featured human regions — based upon human utilization, such as agricultural activities, mining, sericulture, etc. — and formed the foundation stones for the development of such fields as human geography, economic geography, urban geography, and political geography.

Geographical studies may be surveys of a community, a state, a river valley, a climatic region, or a vegetation region. Regardless of the type of region selected or of the size of the region, the method of geographical research in regional units is quite standard. It consists of mapping, surveying, and observing two sets of landscape phenomena: (1) the natural landscape — rivers, climate, land forms, soils, vegetation, minerals, etc.; and (2) the cultural landscape — man-made factors such as farms, crops, manufactures, houses, cities, highways, etc. The studies usually summarize and explain the relationships between man and his environment, and they may, and usually do, go one step further to indicate man's errors and to suggest better ways of using the land. Comparisons and relationships with other regions are generally included, and the geographer adds the time element by indicating the trends and the processes of change in the environment and the human use of the environment. One of the principal postulates of the geographers is that the welfare and progress of mankind are dependent in no small degree upon mankind's ability to understand nature and to make wise utilization of the earth's resources. Their work then is to evaluate the natural environment in regional units and in terms of its use to man. As new methods of research and new instruments for research have evolved, the work of the geographer and the conclusions which he reaches have had ever wider approval and utilization.

One of the most succinct statements concerning the philosophy of the new human geography and the new regional geography is that of Finch and Trewartha of the University of Wisconsin. Both are members of the Association of American Geographers; and both have made large contributions in the field of regional geography. In a college textbook which is widely used they have said:

Within the last few decades a growing tendency has developed among geographers to abandon the notion of environmental relationships as the one principal focus of geographical interest and to return to the traditional theme of the science, with emphasis upon a study of the earth's regions. Both on the continent and in the United States this trend is strongly in evidence. What plants are to the botanist, governments to the political scientist, and heavenly bodies to the astronomer so the earth's regions are to the geographer. The surface of the earth may be thought of as composed of a mosaic of regions, differing from one another in their natural and man-made (cultural) features. In other words, each region has individuality or distinctiveness by reason of the kinds and arrangements of the features that occupy its surface. To delimit these regions, to describe and explain their distinctive characteristics, and to understand the bonds of connection between them is the field of geography.[2]

[2] J. C. Finch and G. T. Trewartha, *Elements of Geography* (New York: McGraw-Hill Book Co., 1937), pp. 4-5.

To illustrate the type of work which geographers have done, the following regional maps of the United States are presented. The first map, Physical Divisions of the United States by Fenneman, shows the eight major physical divisions which Fenneman and others considered to be the logical parts of the United

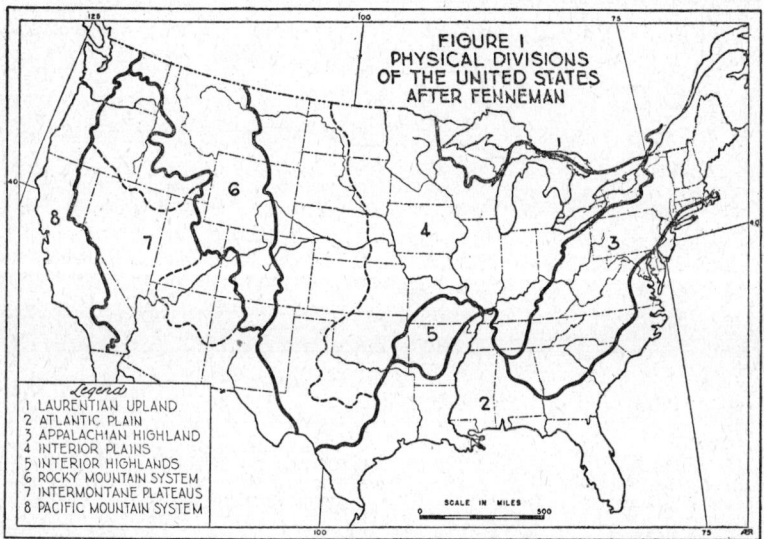

States based upon the geologic structure and the principal topographic features. The map was produced by a committee of the Association of American Geographers whose aim was to produce a map that ". . . would be useful in the consideration of the effects of topography on human affairs."[3] The results of their work (Figure 1) can be seen in many studies in other fields, and in the wide acceptance of the regions by geographers. Figure 2 is one of many maps of the climates of the United States. Renner's map is used because it is simple, and because it is similar to most other climatic maps. Figure 3 is a classification of the major soil types of the United States according to regions.

[3] N. M. Fenneman, "Physical Divisions of the United States," *Annals of The Association of American Geographers*, VI (1916), pp. 22, 23.

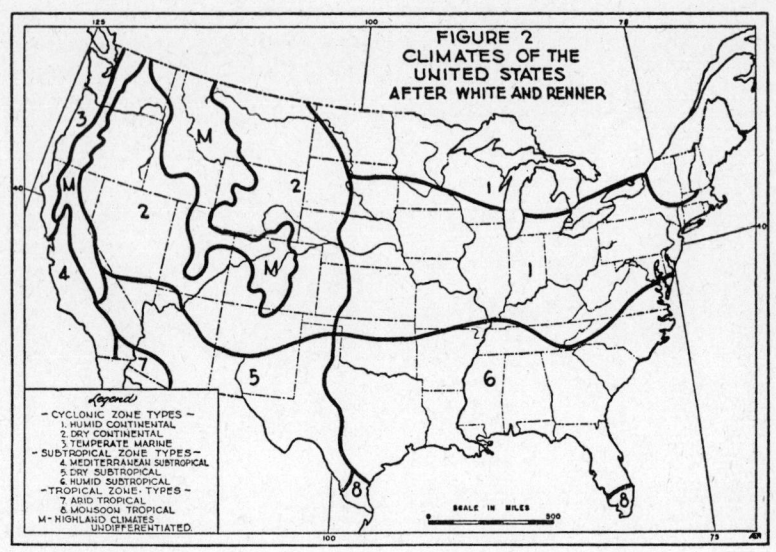

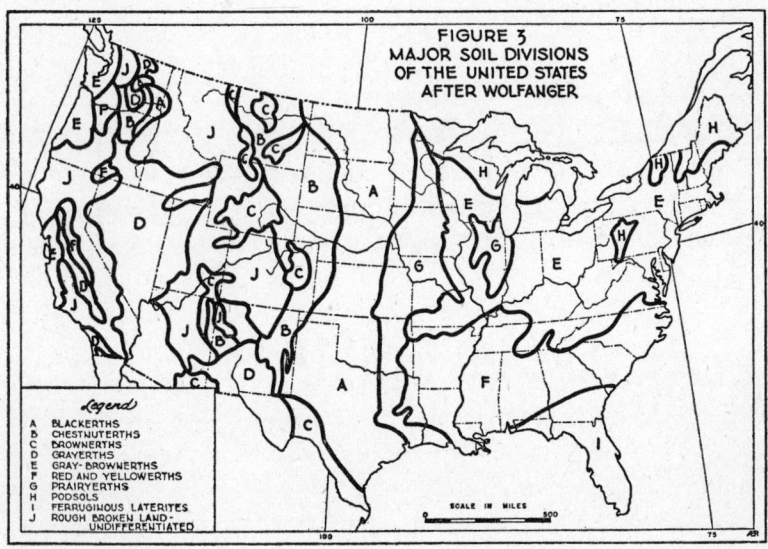

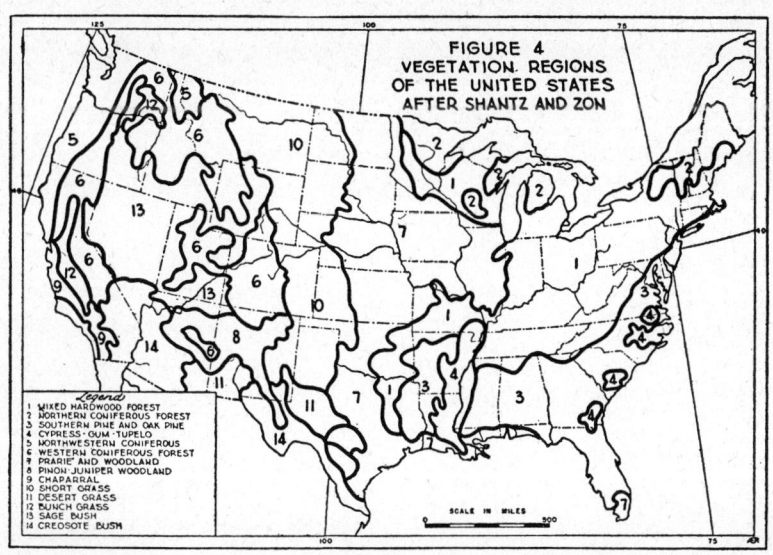

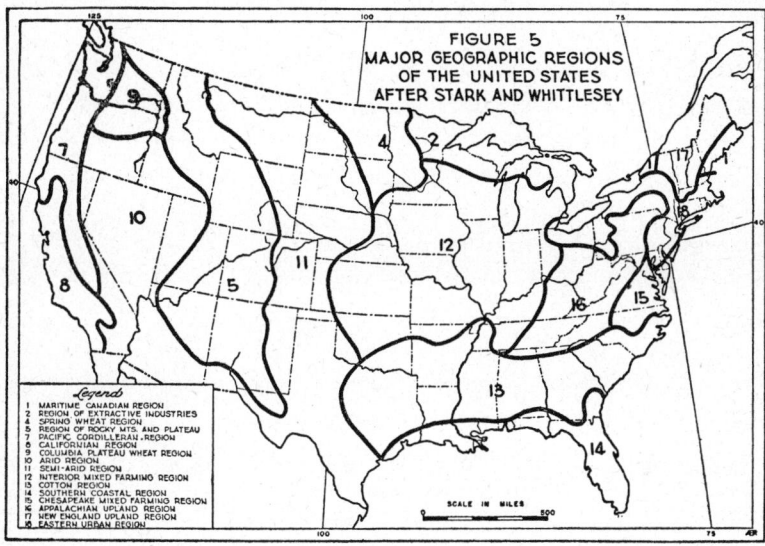

[19]

Figure 4 shows a regional classification of the major types of vegetation found in the United States. The close relationship between soils, climate, and vegetation is shown in the three maps last mentioned. Figure 5 is an attempt to present general geographic regions. In each area the principal factor, whether soils, agriculture, climate, or topography, is used to name the region. This group of maps, produced largely by geographers, gives some idea of the vast amount of research work that has been done in the natural sciences to survey and to describe the natural setting of American life. They point up the fact that it is almost impossible to describe the natural setting without thinking in terms of regions. The close relationship between all of these studies gives stability to the various pieces of research.

The essence of the regional idea in geography, then, is that the land is varied, and that it can best be studied in terms of its variety. Also, the activities of man are closely related to environment, and this means that human activities ought to be studied in terms of regions.

Economics and Regionalism

For the past two centuries the major interest of the economists has been the constructing and testing of a set of theories and principles which deal with the wealth-getting activities of man. To many in other fields of study, the science of economics has appeared as an unusually abstract area, an area in which ordinary words like goods, rent, demand, supply, and value took on deep and eccentric meanings. The classical tradition in economics has not, however, kept the economists from studying society in a realistic manner and with realistic methods. One such approach in the field of economics which emphasizes the new realism in the field is the regional approach.

It has already been remarked that some geographers take the field of economic or commercial geography as a special field. Some of these economic geographers have entered this synthetical area from economics. This situation undoubtedly grows out of the fact that land is one of the principal factors of production, and it necessarily follows that an economist is interested in geography. There is a close relation between the nature of environments and the production of commodities and the transportation of goods. Economists have widely accepted certain basic assumptions relative to the use of land by mankind. The explanation of the major transportation routes of the United States, the systems of communication which have evolved here, and the principal types of commerce and the direction and flow of commerce are examples of the kind of phenomena which economists use to explain their ideas. Economists have long discussed various types of regions such as marginal lands, self-sufficing regions, trading or commercial regions, manufacturing regions, and submarginal regions.

The economist is basically interested in wealth. This means he is interested in the production, distribution, and consumption of material, useful goods, and hence he must take into consideration not only human caprice in terms of demand but the actualities of what nature has for human satisfactions and realizations. Economists are greatly interested in what Zimmerman calls resource patterns, which he defines as

combinations which function as systems. Such a combination may consist of coal, iron, electricity, scientific knowledge, mechanized agriculture and other corollaries. Culture patterns, in general, are adapted to resource patterns, but culture must also be viewed as a part of a resource pattern. Finally, economic systems are parts of culture patterns, namely, those parts which are specifically concerned with material civilization, particularly with making a living. Resource patterns and culture patterns and economic systems together form the basis of human existence.[4]

Thus the world is divided into economic regions on the basis of resource patterns, which, while not determining, have close relationships with the cultural superstructure of attitudes, folkways, mores, and ethical standards.

[4] E. W. Zimmerman, *World Resources and Industries* (New York: Harper and Brothers, 1933), p. 139.

The economic regionalist approaches his study of society from the vantage point of human needs, human demands, and human traits, but he interprets and studies mankind's efforts realistically in terms of the resources or materials which any given segment of mankind has at hand. Many studies have been made by economists which show the diversities which exist because of regional characteristics. For example, some regions have clung to certain types of economic activities long after there is a demand for the goods produced or long after another region has begun to produce them more efficiently, with the result of economic inbalance and social disruption in lagging regions. It has been proved that there are considerable variances in the real wages of workers throughout the United States. It may be possible to encourage workers to work for less in order to lure a given economic activity to one region from another region. Again and again it has been proved that the availability of resources and the location with respect to markets have been factors which produced a great industry such as the steel industry or the automobile industry. The study of such phenomena by economists is indicative of the growing realism in the field of economics. They have become aware of the regional decentralization of enormous national industries and businesses. Almost every national firm has branch offices in the major metropolitan centers of the United States. Financial structures such as the Federal Reserve System of the United States are based upon regional needs and characteristics.

Figures 6 and 7 are illustrative of the regional work of the economists, although it must be admitted that the economists have produced materials which geographers and other social scientists would find interesting and valuable. Figure 6 is a map showing the manufacturing regions of the United States. It shows that there is one enormous region with subregions and with outlying districts. Figure 7 shows the agricultural regions of the United States. This map indicates the close relationship between the economic region and the resource pattern. If this

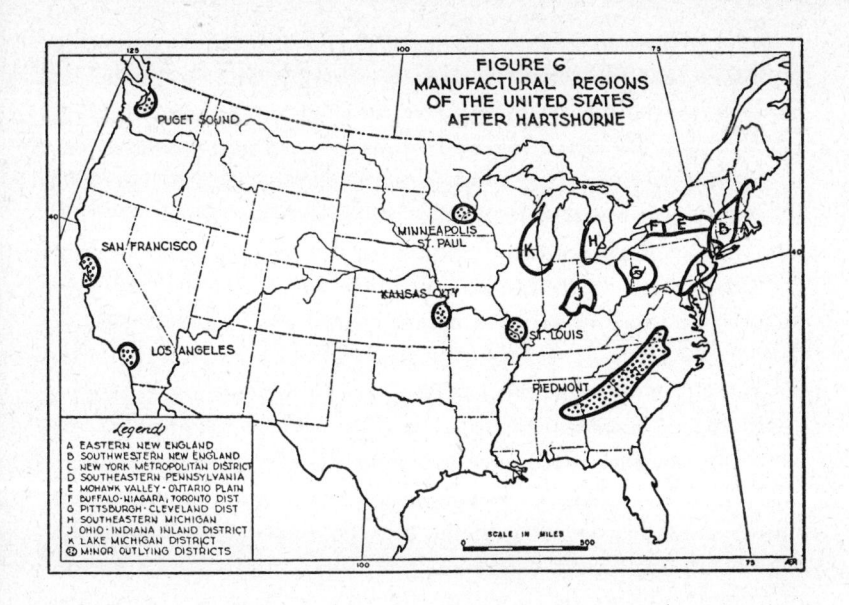

FIGURE 6
MANUFACTURAL REGIONS OF THE UNITED STATES AFTER HARTSHORNE

Legend
A EASTERN NEW ENGLAND
B SOUTHWESTERN NEW ENGLAND
C NEW YORK METROPOLITAN DISTRICT
D SOUTHEASTERN PENNSYLVANIA
E MOHAWK VALLEY - ONTARIO PLAIN
F BUFFALO-NIAGARA, TORONTO DIST
G PITTSBURGH - CLEVELAND DIST
H SOUTHEASTERN MICHIGAN
J OHIO - INDIANA INLAND DISTRICT
K LAKE MICHIGAN DISTRICT
⊕ MINOR OUTLYING DISTRICTS

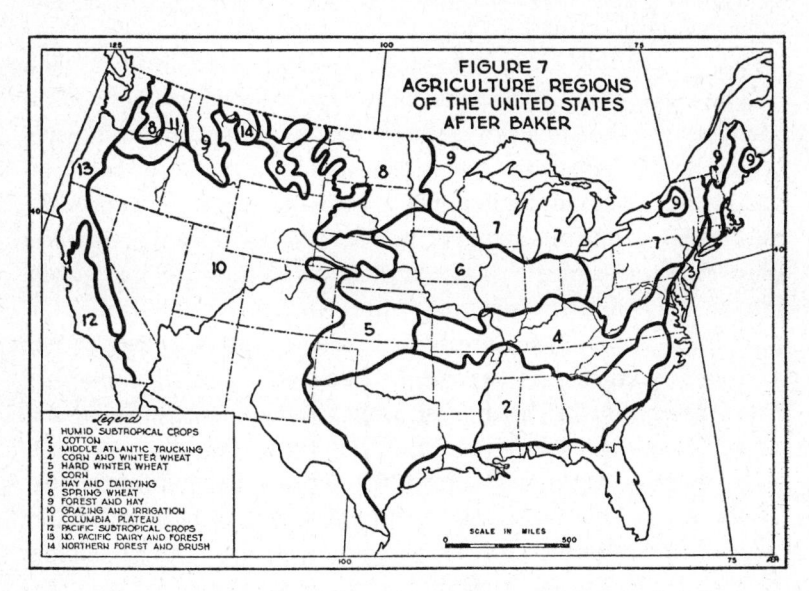

FIGURE 7
AGRICULTURE REGIONS OF THE UNITED STATES AFTER BAKER

Legend
1 HUMID SUBTROPICAL CROPS
2 COTTON
3 MIDDLE ATLANTIC TRUCKING
4 CORN AND WINTER WHEAT
5 HARD WINTER WHEAT
6 CORN
7 HAY AND DAIRYING
8 SPRING WHEAT
9 FOREST AND HAY
10 GRAZING AND IRRIGATION
11 COLUMBIA PLATEAU
12 PACIFIC SUBTROPICAL CROPS
13 NO. PACIFIC DAIRY AND FOREST
14 NORTHERN FOREST AND BRUSH

[23]

map be compared with the maps of the geographers it is readily apparent that the soils, climate, topography, and vegetation of an area are important in determining what will or can be grown there. Thus the great cereal regions of corn and wheat are in the plains regions with moderate rainfall and rich soils, and without much forest vegetation. Hay and dairying are centralized in the northeastern region near the metropolitan manufacturing areas where the soils are thin and can most profitably be used for hay and pasture but there is sufficient moisture. These maps help as no other media can help to explain the close relationships between the various social sciences.

What the economic regionalists are doing is giving roots to economic studies. They are assaying the resources of regions, analyzing their productive capacities in terms of human capabilities and desires, discussing the economic problems of the region, and applying economic principles toward the solution of human problems in the various regions.

Political Science and Regionalism

The study of politics and social control through laws is necessarily a very human study. The myriad factors which influence people to act in certain ways in formulating public opinion, in voting, in campaigning, in defending their interests — economic and social — and many other political factors can only be explained in terms of the total complex in which people live. This means that political scientists must recognize the setting of political activity if they are to be realistic. And they have done so. Their studies of American politics which deal with federalism, sectionalism, localism, and centralization and planning are filled with references to and emphases upon the environments — cultural and natural — in which people live. Turner, the historian of sectionalism, wrote, "I think it not too much to say that in party conventions as well as in Congress the outcome of deliberations bears a striking resemblance to treaties between sections, suggestive of treaties between European nations in

THE SOCIAL SCIENCES

diplomatic congresses."[5] The long struggle between the states and the federal government for power during the nineteenth century is also indicative of the political feelings and activities of parts of the country. Merriam and Gosnell, in a discussion of the meaning of sectionalism, wrote:

Social interests, whether economic, racial, or religious, may center in particular territorial areas and thus add the sectional feeling to the group sentiment. Where this is true the sentiment strikes deeply into the party soil, and party action becomes more significant. If race, class and geography combine, we have a very powerful combination such as the "Solid South."[6]

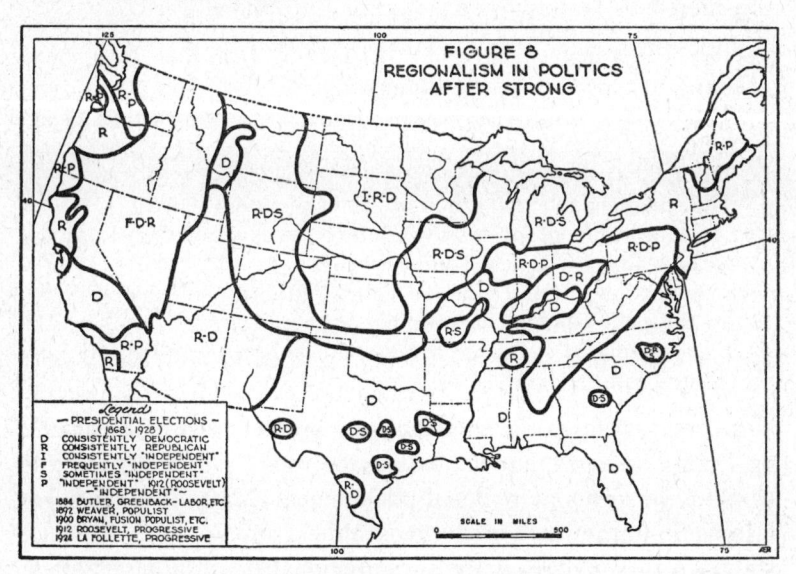

FIGURE 8
REGIONALISM IN POLITICS
AFTER STRONG

Figure 8 illustrates regionalism in American politics. It shows that groups of states tend to vote consistently Democratic, Independent, or Republican. This is a characteristic of the United States, and it has been true since the founding of the nation.

[5] F. J. Turner, *The Significance of Sections in American History* (New York: Henry Holt & Co., 1932), p. 41.
[6] C. E. Merriam and H. F. Gosnell, *The American Party System* (New York: The Macmillan Company, 1940), p. 79.

The political regionalists are not interested in perpetuating sectionalism. Sectionalism implies an overemphasis upon the section at the cost of the rest of the nation. Regionalism means looking at the nation from the national point of view but recognizing the diversity of culture and land. The political regionalists hope to produce a functional unity within the nation which will not destroy the necessary diversity of its parts. In its comprehensive report on regional planning and government — written very largely by political scientists — the National Resources Committee declared that the problems of the nation must be considered as regional problems for the following reasons:

1. The increasingly clear realization of the inadequacy of single states to carry out all planning programs.
2. The development of an extensive interstate coöperation movement.
3. The rise of metropolitan planning.
4. The emergence of two group-of-States planning regions.
5 The establishment of more than 100 types of Federal regional areas dealing with field administration.
6. The creation of the Tennessee Valley Authority and the proposals for the establishment of other like authorities.
7. The pressure of economic distress and unbalance in various agricultural-industrial areas.[7]

The demarcation of the chief land-use problem region illustrated by Figure 9 shows that the National Resources Committee was thinking in terms of regional phenomena. Notice the close relationship to the work of the geographers and economists which shows in this map. The political regionalists who have shown an interest in and contributed to national social planning are basing no small part of their work on the work of the geographers and economists and other regionalists.

The political scientists are clearly aware that our regions are realities in American life. Historical studies show the trends over a century and a half of national life to be of such a char-

[7] *Regional Factors in National Planning* (Washington: U. S. Government Printing Office, 1935), p. vi.

acter that one can predict almost certainly how various regions will vote on a given issue. Politics today reflect the stamp of regional economic and social interests. The South and the Northeast are definitely more "internationalist" than the Middle West. The continuing struggle over the poll tax always

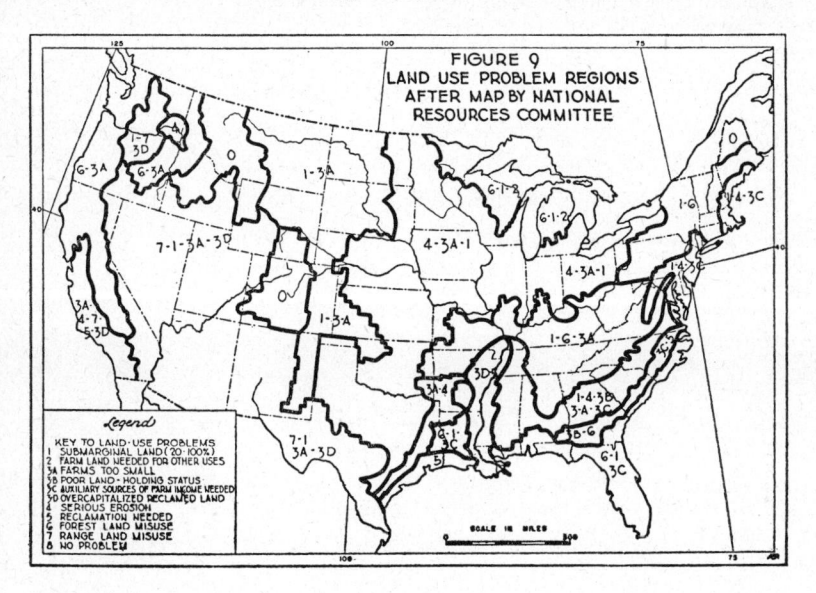

FIGURE 9
LAND USE PROBLEM REGIONS AFTER MAP BY NATIONAL RESOURCES COMMITTEE

KEY TO LAND-USE PROBLEMS
1 SUBMARGINAL LAND (20-100%)
2 FARM LAND NEEDED FOR OTHER USES
3A FARMS TOO SMALL
3B POOR LAND - HOLDING STATUS
3C AUXILIARY SOURCES OF FARM INCOME NEEDED
3D OVERCAPITALIZED RECLAIMED LAND
4 SERIOUS EROSION
5 RECLAMATION NEEDED
6 FOREST LAND MISUSE
7 RANGE LAND MISUSE
8 NO PROBLEM

shows that the South has been adamant and united in the Senate and House of Representatives against a law to prohibit using the poll tax as prerequisite to voting.

Thus, the political regionalists recognize the relation of culture and landscape to politics. They utilize the studies of geographers, sociologists, and economists to bolster their conclusions, and to seek government action to solve the nation's problems. One book has been written urging the destruction of the local powers of the many states and the substitution of federal regions consisting of groups of states.[8] It is argued that this would reduce the number of local governments and thereby

[8] W. Y. Elliott, *The Need for Constitutional Reform* (New York: McGraw-Hill Book Co., 1935).

increase efficiency by establishing nonpolitical federal administrative agencies. While there are many faults to be found with such proposals, one can detect in them an earnest attempt to solve the persistent political problems of the nation in terms of national welfare, but in line with regional realities.

ANTHROPOLOGY AND REGIONALISM

In the concept of the culture area can be found the anthropological approach to regionalism. This concept had its genesis in the frontier efforts of American anthropologists to classify the cultures of Indian tribes occupying the American continents before the coming of the white man. Lacking written records, the scholar in the field of anthropology had to rely upon excavations which produced tools, cooking equipment, fragments of wearing apparel, and weapons. It was not long until the diversity of the various Indian groups was delimited into regions or areas in which certain customs, habits, and tools were common. As Wissler says, "If . . . we take all traits into simultaneous consideration and shift our point of view to the social, or tribal units, we are able to form fairly definite groups according to their culture traits." [9] That is, in an area in which a characteristic form of dwelling, for example, is found, there would also be characteristic complexes describing clothing, food, and items of nonmaterial culture, such as ceremonies. Wissler demonstrated the essential truth of this proposition in his book on American Indians just quoted and in subsequent studies by working out a division of indigenous North American culture into nine regional patterns, using a classification of nine categories which he says are universal. Figure 10 is Wissler's map.

Wissler's work on the American Indian was used here to introduce the anthropologist's concept of the region. There is some variance among the anthropologists themselves, many of whom are severe critics of Wissler. Odum and Moore, in their

[9] Clark Wissler, *The American Indian* (New York: Oxford University Press, 1938), p. 218.

study of regionalism, have pointed out and summarized these criticisms by other anthropologists.[10] It has been said that Wissler's view of culture areas is lifeless and inorganic, that the

FIGURE 10
CULTURE AREAS OF THE NORTH AMERICAN INDIAN AFTER WISSLER

areas are highly indefinite, that the concept lacks a time depth which eliminates the idea of evolution and progress. Still, these criticisms do not invalidate the idea that culture takes place in

[10] H. W. Odum and H. E. Moore, *American Regionalism: A Cultural-Historical Approach to National Integration* (New York: Henry Holt, 1938), p. 218.

patches or areas. Culture is always defined and characterized with reference to certain places such as Athens, Alexandria, the South, Weimar, White Russia, or New England. What the regional anthropologists are mainly contending is that culture always exists in some place, and they take as one of their tasks the tracing and the delimitation of culture in terms of place. They admit that the limits of a regional culture do not become absolute and precise. Rather, the boundaries are zones of transition, and there is intermingling as the result of marriage, war, migration, and human caprice. Their studies merge with human geography, sociology, human ecology, and geology, but they make a significant contribution by taking into account many factors of culture in an area which the other fields usually pass by. They are interested in the totality of culture in a place at a time.[11]

SOCIOLOGY AND REGIONALISM

Since a vast amount of work has already been done on the sociologist's concept of regionalism by Odum and Moore, the basis of this discussion will follow their research embodied in their study, *American Regionalism*.[12] According to Odum and Moore, the sociologists have taken several approaches to regionalism. There is the regional conception held by Mukerjee which would emphasize the classification of social types in terms of harmony with physical environment, or the "regional balance of man." [13] He appeals for a broader sociology which, while recognizing the geographers' and anthropologists' contributions, would attempt to correlate all the factors. This concept is quite widely held by regional sociologists, but others attempt to make the work realistic by using the concept to attack such problems as urban-rural competition and imbalance, regional maladjustment, metropolitan problems, and national integra-

[11] *Ibid.*
[12] *Cit. supra*, n. 10.
[13] R. Mukerjee, *Regional Sociology* (New York: The Century Co., 1926), p. viii.

tion. Hundreds of articles and dozens of major studies have been published on these sociological problems. It would be impossible to list all of them here, but some can be discussed.

One of these studies has attracted national attention. It is Odum's *Southern Regions of the United States*. After surveying the natural and human resources of the South, Odum proceeds to make recommendations for the regeneration and development of the region. He points out that there is an amazing ignorance of the various regions of the United States, and that there is needed a fundamental understanding of the diversity of folk cultures in America before the society can be reordered and regenerated.[14] The reordering of society ought to be in terms of the regional cultures and their backgrounds.

The rise of the great cities in America has produced an emphasis upon their study and survey by sociologists, in particular Metropolitan regionalism emphasizes the tremendous influence of a large city upon a large area known as the hinterland. The hinterland is dependent upon the great city, and the great city is dependent upon a host of smaller urban centers and rural areas. Figure 11 illustrates metropolitan regionalism. It is a map of metropolitan regions delimited by R. D. McKenzie on the basis of influence of great cities of the United States.

The final stage of sociological research in regional phenomena is perhaps best illustrated by the work of Odum. Figure 12 shows how Odum delimited a group of socio-economic regions of the United States. He recognizes that the boundaries are transitional. He used state boundaries because of the importance of state governments in national life. This group of regions has gained wide acceptance in the United States by scholars in many fields.

Regional planning has been discussed briefly earlier in this chapter, but the sociologist's contribution and thinking on the meaning of regional social planning are worth mentioning here.

[14] H. W. Odum, *Southern Regions of the United States* (Chapel Hill: University of North Carolina Press, 1936), pp. 251–253.

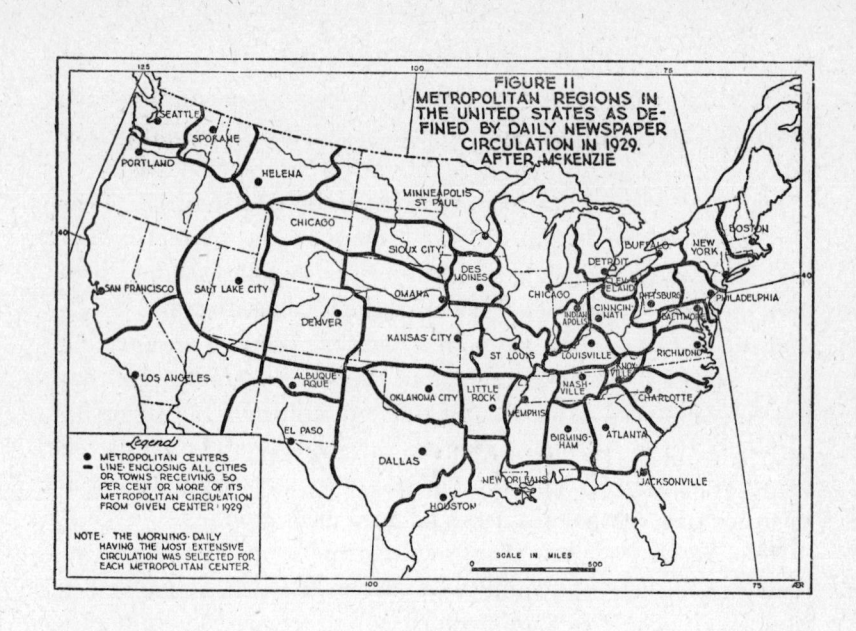

FIGURE 11. METROPOLITAN REGIONS IN THE UNITED STATES AS DEFINED BY DAILY NEWSPAPER CIRCULATION IN 1929. AFTER McKENZIE.

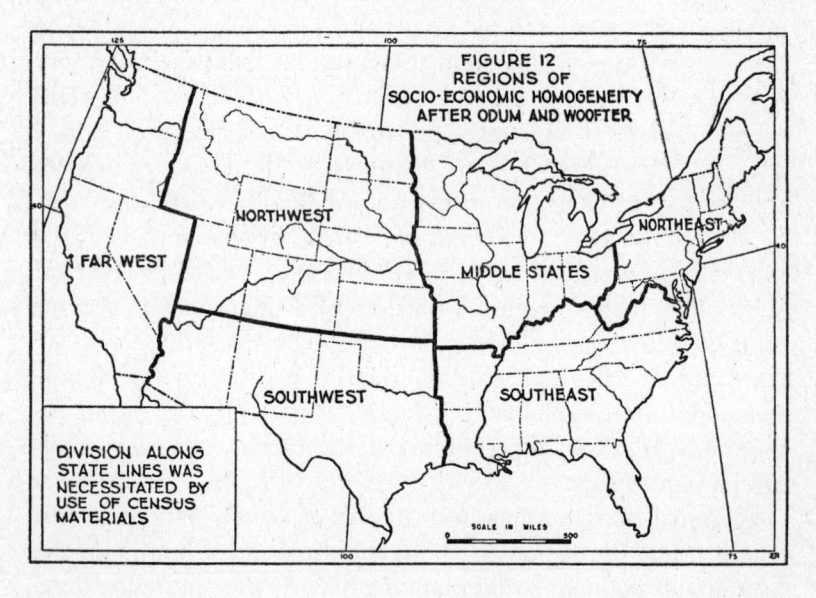

FIGURE 12. REGIONS OF SOCIO-ECONOMIC HOMOGENEITY AFTER ODUM AND WOOFTER.

THE SOCIAL SCIENCES

The classic statement of the sociological approach to social planning through regions is that by Odum which follows:

1. The sociological approach must be an analysis of the problems involved. This is a problem in social analysis. . . . 2. It must be an integration of these problems in a coordinated, balanced, picture. This is a problem in social synthesis. . . . 3. Equilibrium is the keynote to social planning. This is the problem of social balance. . . . 4. The transitional society between epochs or between crises or between changing cultures is the key problem to equilibrium. . . . 5. Therefore, from the sociological viewpoint, the cultural, the folk, the regional, the national myth, the time-space relationships are fundamental elements transcending economic integration, which is the first essential of emergency reconstruction. . . . 6. The sociological approach is in contrast to that of political philosophy, exclusive economic planning, subjective ideologies, abstract utopias, the perfectionists' panaceas, and all of the specialized isms. . . . 7. There must grow out of the sociological approach basic principles and framework upon which administrators can build an enduring plan susceptible of flexibility and change. The sociologist does not perfect the plan, neither does he attempt to administer it.[15]

Thus, regionalism in the field of sociology looks both to an explanation and an evaluation of society in terms of the several factors: race, folkways, origins, history, geography, politics, and economics. It is the hope of the sociologists that their regional studies comprehend the nearest approximation to a synthesis of studies, methods, and concepts, to the end that the long-run welfare of the social order may be sustained.

LITERARY AND AESTHETIC REGIONALISM

Although literary and aesthetic regionalism is a much more subjective and intuitive field of study, certainly it cannot be overlooked in the general study of regionalism or in the study of the meaning of regionalism in American life. Very often the best clue to an understanding of the life of a people is the liter-

[15] H. W. Odum, "A Sociological Approach to National Social Planning," *Sociology and Social Research*, vol. 19, No. 4, p. 306 (March-April, 1935).

ature and arts which have grown out of the life of a people. That the life and environment in which a writer or an artist lives casts an influence upon his work is a common assumption among literary critics and students of art and music. This is one aspect of the meaning of literary and aesthetic regionalism. The other aspect is that much of the artistry that has portrayed American life has found its color and flavor because of the vast diversity that is here. These two aspects are not inseparable. They can be illustrated. Mark Twain portrayed his region and his time in his novels, but he also wrote of other places as a Missourian would. His novels *Huckleberry Finn* and *Tom Sawyer* tell of life on the Mississippi River, but his *Innocents Abroad* tells of life in Europe as a Missourian would view it. There is the regionalism that springs from the life of the artist and the regionalism which controls the plot, the characters, and the color of the drama, novel, or short story. Literary and aesthetic regionalism is not the same as localism or provincialism. It does not mean that a writer or artist accepts the past as an absolute by fixing on some point in the past or some local spot in the present and retreating into it to live it over and over again.

Three early American writers illustrate literary regionalism which shows the control of an environment over writers. These are Washington Irving, James Fenimore Cooper, and William Cullen Bryant. Irving was steeped in the legends of the early Dutch settlers of New York, and he spent years learning the geography and life on the Hudson River. Later he embodied the spirit and feelings of his youth in such masterpieces as *Knickerbocker's History of New York*, and the *Legend of Sleepy Hollow*. Cooper, on the other hand, lived nearer the frontier during his boyhood, in close touch with the forest and the pioneers and the Indians. How else could he have produced such colorful tales as *The Last of the Mohicans* or the other Leatherstocking Tales? Bryant came of the puritan tradition in rural Massachusetts, and his life was strongly influenced by his home and church, so that his poetry echoes the spirituality and morality of his day and place.

The literary regionalist who uses history or the present social scene as the foundation for his work is more than an antiquarian or someone interested only in picturesqueness. The real regionalist is one who can secure a fine organic sense of the flow and pulsation of life in the various areas which humans inhabit. In the best sense, the literary regionalist presents a segment of a total national life. The great novels of the various regions pulsate not only because they portray brilliantly a scene of American life, but also because they show the relation of the region to the whole. Of such scope are Edna Ferber's *Cimarron*, Mary Ellen Chase's *Uplands* and *Windswept*, John Steinbeck's *Grapes of Wrath*, and Margaret Mitchell's *Gone With the Wind*. These are great novels because they have a regional setting which is a *part* of a total national culture. The regionalist tries to present the human spirit in relation to the immediate environment through the use of the cultural riches of any given region.

Out of the heart and history of America have come the ballads of the plains and the spirituals of the South. It was the pioneer who carried the ballads westward and who used them at the campfire and in the home. They have remained a part of the musical tradition of the West and Middle West. In the South the Negroes developed and fostered their deeply rich and colorful religious songs. Without widespread printing of hymnals each of these groups sustained a musical tradition for a century or more with constant use of their music in their churches, their social gatherings, and in their work. Yet the balladry and the spirituals are part of the whole American scene, making it richer and finer because such music was the heritage of the builders of the nation in their work and in their play.

To the artist, the dramatist, or the novelist, regional portraiture is more than the portrayal of the local oddities or curiosities; it implies understanding, analysis, and interpretation of life. The regionalist realizes that he is selecting a part of a larger entity for his artistry, and he selects that part because he has lived it or because he has become a student of it.

SUMMARY

Here, then, is a summary of the work of the social scientists and the artists who have taken the regional approach to an understanding of American society. There is considerable overlapping in their various fields, and there is a close dependence of one science upon another. Geographers, anthropologists, economists, political scientists, and sociologists now use the regional method of social survey and research widely. The essence of their work and the theme of their philosophy are apparent in their characterization of American life in terms of its areal diversities resulting from implanted cultures in a wide variety of natural environments. They see America as a national entity in political union, in a total frame of reference, but they see its richness resulting from its diverse landscapes and cultures. They take as their task the interpretation of social life, and they see social life in terms of social settings. Out of the flow of their studies comes the meaning of regionalism for each field of social study. Each makes a contribution in terms of the tools of the field of study and the chief interests of the scholars. They are all at the task of interpreting one of the most complex areas of human living that the world has ever seen. That there is diversity in their delineation of regions is a good thing, for it widens the potentialities for viewing a social scene. Regionalism refutes sectionalism, nationalism, and provincialism. Inherent in the work of the regionalists is the conception of cultural change, progress, and realism. In place of the narrow competitiveness of sectionalism and nationalism, the regionalists envisage reciprocal relations. In place of the ignorance of provincialism, the regionalists see education, light, and interpretation.

The few studies of American life which have been presented here are but samples of dozens of studies, but they suffice to show that the nation is diverse in landscape and culture. Other facets of American life which could have been presented with these and which deserve mention are such ordinary things as the diverse ways in which the English language is spoken in the various regions, the variety of clothing worn, the sports of the nation, the culinary habits of the various regions, and the architecture of the nation.

An excellent statement of the meaning and significance of regionalism is that of Lewis Mumford:

> At a period when the uniformities of the machine civilization were being overstressed, regionalism served to emphasize compensatory organic elements; above all, those differences that arise out of geographic, historic, and cultural peculiarities. In its recognition of the region as the basic configuration in human life; in its acceptance of natural diversities as well as natural associations and uniformities; in its recognition of the region as a permanent sphere of cultural influences and as a center of economic activities, as well as an implicit geographic fact — here lies the vital common element in the regionalist movement.[16]

But regionalism in the social sciences and as a method for interpreting the life of a nation has important implications. It is a tool for social planning, for government administration, for business organization, and for viewing the life of a nation in a more realistic manner. Such a movement has in it the vitality that is needed to hold the fabric of the nation together, and to mend it for future generations. Such a conception of American life as the regionalists are presenting and have already presented offers much to Americans in viewing their history, their economy, and their total culture, and in planning their education.

American Regionalism and the Social Studies

In most American schools the social-studies program draws its content very largely from the social sciences. The social-studies teacher is trained in the social sciences, and the text-

---

[16] Lewis Mumford, *The Culture of Cities* (New York: Harcourt, Brace & Co., 1938), p. 305.

books are written by social scientists. Moreover, the membership of the national committees, which have influenced social-studies programs and instruction in America has consisted largely of social scientists and educators grounded in those fields. Throughout the literature on the social studies are statements by prominent leaders which give evidence of the dependence of the social studies upon the social sciences for content and for organization.

Social research which takes the regional approach has now come to such maturity that it can no longer be overlooked by those who make the social-studies programs of American schools. The findings of regional research are affecting government planning, business, government administration, and, to an increasing extent, education. It has already been pointed out that to some extent education has felt the impact of the new regionalism, and that many new studies have appeared which stress the implications of regionalism for education. Many colleges and universities have already altered their courses in social sciences to include the new regional research, and in many instances courses have been introduced which take the regional approach entirely.

The social-studies programs of American schools take their bearings from the character of American society. This fact makes it imperative that, if youth is to receive the best possible understanding of American society, and if the schools are to reflect the needs and problems of society, then the social-studies programs must present youth with the regional nature of American life. That is, the environment of education ought to influence educational content and practice more than it now does. This ideal is one toward which many schools have striven, but the present curriculums of the schools need considerable revision if the ideal is to be achieved. It is believed that schools in the various regions of the United States ought to attune themselves more realistically to the life which surrounds them and which supports them. This would mean that the regional portraiture and the regional problems would be an important part of the program of education in the schools of any given region. This idea has been sounded by many educators and by many regionalists, but as yet it has not been extensively implemented or realized.

It has been said that the general welfare of society is the test of educational effectiveness. To some degree this is true, and it offers an excellent ideal toward which all education in the common schools of a great democracy should strive. Since many of the problems of America are regional in nature, and since the solutions to these problems are being sought in terms of regions by competent scholars, administrators, and industrialists, it seems that schools ought also to make a contribution to the solution of regional problems and the creation of regional welfare. Schools do not administer or plan programs of social progress, except as they present effective information to youth and as they become important agencies in the life of a community or region. But there is room for the schools to make an excellent contribution to regional well-being, as has been suggested previously, by presenting youth with the understanding of regional resources, problems, and potentialities. At least such knowledge is vital for the exercising of a competent citizenship through understanding the alternative courses of action which a people can take. Moreover, the educational policy of most of America's common schools is based upon the theory that schools are educating youth so that youth can make a significant contribution to its own self-realization. It is taken for granted that the individual is an important factor in life in this democracy, and it is the purpose of education, in part, to prepare individuals to make intelligent social, economic, political, and moral choices in life. Since America's is a diverse culture, American youth needs to understand it as a diverse culture; youth can make the best adaptation to its environment through understanding the regional character of American life.

Two closely related objectives of education are discussed in the preceding paragraph: the needs of society and the needs of youth. A good society cannot exist unless individuals are free and effective; and individuals cannot be free and effective in a poor or disorganized society.

From these implications of regionalism and the regional nature of American life come the next steps in this discussion. A region has been selected for analysis as to character, problems, and needs, and a survey of the teaching of the social studies in the schools of this region has been made to determine to what extent the social-studies programs have acquainted youth with the life and problems of the region. The region — New England — is an old American region, and is recognized as such by many competent scholars and by society in general in America. Following the discussion of the character of New England and the teaching of New England regional life and problems in the social-studies programs of New England schools, a program of content will be organized which is recommended for the youth of New England and a statement of the procedures which might be employed, together with available educational resources.

CHAPTER III

NEW ENGLAND AS AN AMERICAN REGION

NEW ENGLAND is the term commonly used to include the six most northeasterly states of the United States: Maine, New Hampshire, Vermont, Massachusetts, Rhode Island, and Connecticut. But, as William R. Greeley has written, New England

is more than the six northeastern states. It is the ethical region of the New England conscience and of Puritanism. It is an industrial region separate from all other industrial regions, a recreational region of rugged coast, tumbled mountains, crystal streams and lakes, sloping orchards, and white pine forests.[1]

History, culture, economy, geography, and polity combine to make New England a region. It is a distinct entity in the nation. Yet New England is American. It is the home of the "Yankee." Its three centuries have produced national leaders in literature, the arts, and politics, and its great centers of learning and culture are part of the total culture that is America.

The purpose of this chapter is to analyze and to describe the principal factors of New England life and its environment. Five topics will serve as the foci for the discussion: (1) the regional setting and resources; (2) the regional population and cultural heritage; (3) the regional economy; (4) some important regional problems; and (5) recent trends in regional coöperation and integration. The purpose here is to present these factors of New England regional life in terms of the total regional culture.

[1] *New England's Prospect: 1933*, edited by J. K. Wright (New York: American Geographical Society, 1933), p. 406.

SETTING AND RESOURCES

A few minutes with a map of the United States (Figure 13) discloses several significant geographic factors which have influenced the development of New England. Its situation in the extreme northeastern corner of the United States places the region in proximity to the Maritime Provinces of Canada and the Grand Banks, and nearer to Europe than any other American region. The influences which this location have wrought in New England culture are many. New England is a small region, as American regions go, for it comprises but 2 per cent

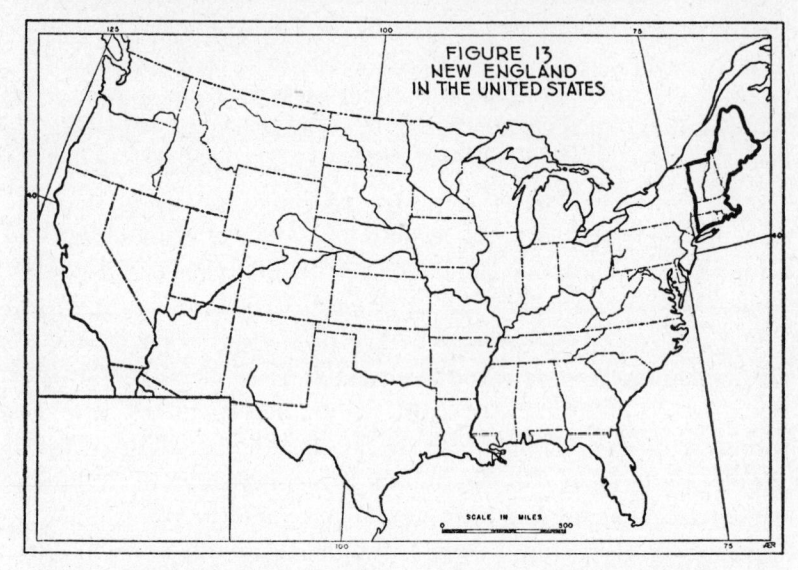

FIGURE 13
NEW ENGLAND
IN THE UNITED STATES

of the land area of the nation. The regional boundaries are quite well defined: the Atlantic Ocean to the east, Long Island Sound to the south, the Hudson-Champlain Valley to the west, and the Canadian border to the north. At times these factors of New England's geography have helped to produce a narrow sectionalism, and, at times, a worldly cosmopolitanism.

The New England landscape is not susceptible to generalization for description. Here are neither vast plains nor continuous plateaus. Here are rough, tumbled, disorganized uplands interspersed with minute river valleys, a multitude of ponds, and several large lakes. Even the coast has its variety: in the southern portion it is usually wide and sandy or marshy; in the north, fiord-like formations appear in Maine, with numerous rocky inlets and islands. The chief physical divisions of New England (Figure 14) are the Coastal Lowlands and Islands, the Eastern Uplands, the White Mountains, the Western Uplands, the Green Mountains, and the valleys of the major rivers. Altitude is the principal criterion used in making such topographic divisions of the region. There is little or no sharp demarcation between one division and another. Usually one is never out of sight of hilly lands in New England, and toward the interior one may view continuous mountains and uplands extending as far as the eye can see in all directions. Mount Greylock in northern Massachusetts, Mount Monadnock in southern New Hampshire, Mount Washington in central New Hampshire, and Mount Katahdin in Maine are examples of vantage points which give views which extend for miles.

New England lies wholly within the humid portion of the United States; everywhere the annual precipitation averages more than 25 inches.[2] In the extreme north the average precipitation annually is about 30 inches, but in the southern portions of the region it ranges from 40 to 45 inches. This is sufficient precipitation to produce a permanent forest and to raise most of the crops which can be grown in a temperate region. The whole region receives snow in the winter months, and the uplands are continuously blanketed for three to four months of the year. Summer temperatures average around 60° throughout the region, with the exception of the uplands and the Maine coast, where the averages are about five degrees

---

[2] All statistics on climate are taken from "Climate and Man," *Yearbook of Agriculture* (Washington: U. S. Dept. of Agriculture, 1942), section on "New England."

44 REGIONALISM AND SOCIAL EDUCATION

lower. In the southern half of the region winter temperatures average about 25°, whereas in the northern half, and in the

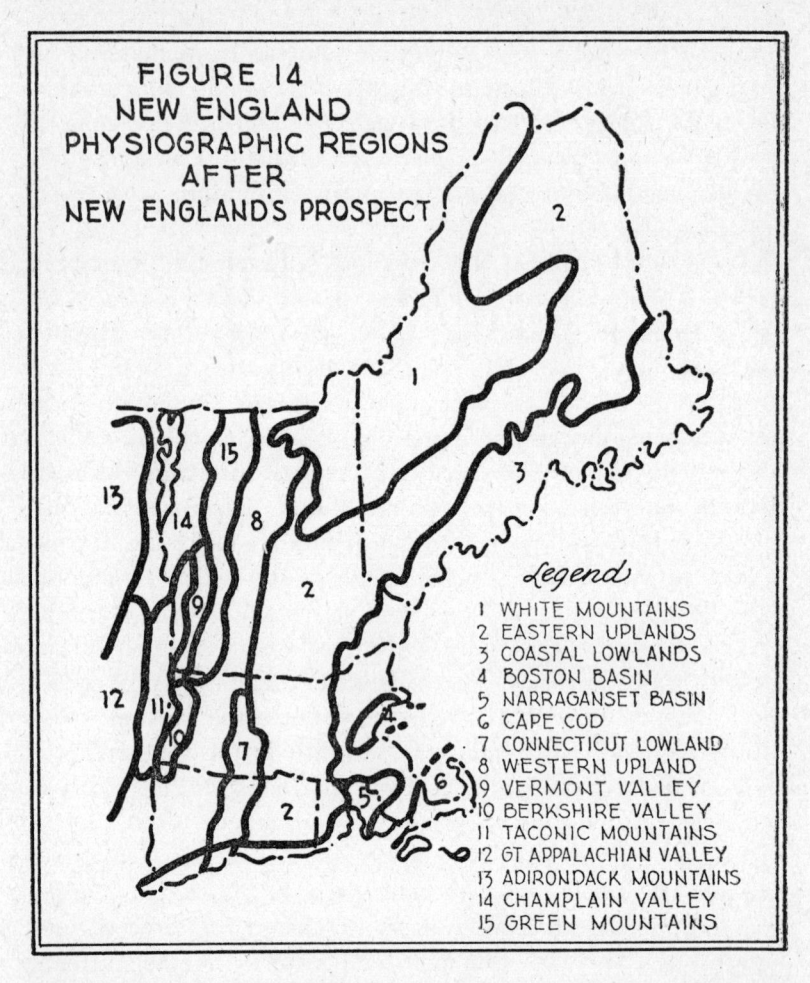

FIGURE 14
NEW ENGLAND
PHYSIOGRAPHIC REGIONS
AFTER
NEW ENGLAND'S PROSPECT

Legend
1 WHITE MOUNTAINS
2 EASTERN UPLANDS
3 COASTAL LOWLANDS
4 BOSTON BASIN
5 NARRAGANSET BASIN
6 CAPE COD
7 CONNECTICUT LOWLAND
8 WESTERN UPLAND
9 VERMONT VALLEY
10 BERKSHIRE VALLEY
11 TACONIC MOUNTAINS
12 GT APPALACHIAN VALLEY
13 ADIRONDACK MOUNTAINS
14 CHAMPLAIN VALLEY
15 GREEN MOUNTAINS

mountains, winter temperatures average 20° or less. The growing season varies from north to south, averaging about 120 days in the north and ranging up to 200 days in the Cape Cod area. Drought rarely threatens New England, although dry seasons often are conducive to devastating forest fires. Hailstorms are occasionally a serious menace to the tobacco crop in Connecticut. Hurricanes are few, but when a hurricane comes in from the southeast, it may be disastrous for life and property. The climate of New England is, on the whole, an excellent one, for it is cool enough in the summer to lure thousands of tourists and summer residents, and snowy enough in the winter to induce thousands to ski on the slopes of the uplands and mountains. New England's climate is one of her most valuable resources.

About 70 per cent of New England is covered by woodland. Yet only a small percentage of the forests are considered valuable for timber or other economic utilization. Thousands of square miles of woodland consist of juniper scrub or birch scrub, and this is often little more than a fire hazard. Much of the woodland is found on abandoned farms and consists of wasteland. The valuable timber is usually associated with the uplands and the northern portion of the region. White pine, spruce, and northern hardwoods, such as oak, beech, and maple, constitute the principal kinds of valuable timber. According to Henry Graves of the Yale School of Forestry, the total amount of saw timber in New England is slightly less than sixty billion board feet.[3] He estimates that the material suited for wood pulp aggregates about two hundred million cords. R. T. Fisher, Director of the Harvard Forest, described the depletion of New England's forests by saying that

in two centuries the people of New England have used up all but a scant two million acres of an original forest covering thirty-nine of the forty million acres included in the six states. Not less than fifteen million of these acres became farm and pasture, of which at least ten million have been abandoned to revert to forest and thus accidentally to produce a supplementary crop of timber, the best of which has now been cut down. There are still about twenty-seven million acres in woodland, but of this more than half is covered with comparatively valueless trees or undesirable species.[4]

[3] *New England's Prospect: 1933*, p. 226.
[4] *Ibid.*, p. 218.

Water is by far the most valuable mineral resource of New England. Streams and reservoirs annually produce more than two million horsepower, and it has been estimated by the New England Regional Planning Commission that another million and a half horsepower could be installed.[5] Most of this water power is employed for the production of approximately three million kilowatts of electric power. Since water power is based ultimately upon the slope of the drainage systems and the continuous supply of rainfall to fill the streams, New England is fortunate. The gradient of the streams, or the location of ponds and lakes in the uplands, makes it possible for men to use the forces of energy of running water for mills and for power plants in the region. It is easy to impound waters for storage purposes almost anywhere in the region because of the narrow valleys that are characteristic and because of the relatively even rainfall that can be depended upon year after year. The inland streams and ponds and lakes of New England are clear and beautiful, and most of them are surrounded by woodland which adds to their scenic beauty. The streams and lakes are important attractions for tourists, for summer residents, and for summer camps. Since the earliest days of settlement, the Atlantic Ocean has been a most valuable and potent resource in the life of New England. It served as a medium of transportation between the earliest coastal settlements and between the settlements and the rest of the world. It was the chief route of the commerce which laid the foundation for New England's future economy. Moreover, it was and is a very important source of food. New England is only a day's run from the fishing area of the Grand Banks, and many kinds of fish and sea foods are gathered close to shore. The ocean is the basis of New England's distinct culinary personality, and today a shore dinner is an enticing experience for Americans from

[5] *Regional Planning, Part III, New England* (Washington: U. S. Government Printing Office, 1936), p. 52.

THE NEW ENGLAND REGION 47

other regions as well as a continuous source of delight among New Englanders.

Marble, granite, sandstone, shale, clay, mica, and high-grade sands and gravels have been profitably extracted from New England's land for more than two centuries. Other valuable mineral resources are found in the region, but none exist in quantities which can be profitably extracted. At one time even iron ore was produced from the bogs near Saugus, Massachusetts, but the opening of richer mines in the Middle West forced the Saugus enterprises out of existence.

Nature did not endow New England with much rich soil. The glacier deposited gravel and rocky materials over the entire region, and boulders are always an annual crop for many New England farmers. In the broader river valleys, level and rich expanses of soil exist as a result of post-glacial deposition and alluviation. Particularly valuable are the soils of the Connecticut and Aroostook valleys. There is scarcely any spot in the region where successful crop agriculture can be practiced without fertilizers. Only one fourth of 1 per cent of the total area of the region is classified by the United States Soil Conservation Service as "excellent for the cultivation of crops." [6] More than 40 per cent of the soils of New England are classified as "essentially incapable of tillage." [7]

New England's resources, while not extremely rich, are of the type which is valuable over a long period of time. Forests can be managed; water resources can be husbanded; and soils can be made to last forever with careful planning. The Atlantic Ocean as a resource for food and transportation remains constant. The building stones are nowhere near exhaustion. The basic resources which New England has are susceptible to many uses, and, with careful planning and wise use, can form the basis for a stable economy indefinitely.

[6] New England Regional Planning Commission, *Economic Conditions of New England* (mimeographed; Boston: The Commission, 1939), p. 4.
[7] *Ibid.*

POPULATION AND CULTURAL HERITAGE

The chief resource of New England is the people. More than eight million inhabit the region, and here are found almost every race and nationality. Heterogeneity characterizes the regional population today. This heterogeneity, however, was not present in colonial New England. It was not until the first quarter of the nineteenth century that layer after layer of new peoples were placed upon the old Anglo-Puritan stock.[8] During the nineteenth century, Europeans came to New England regularly after every revolutionary upheaval. The potato famine of Ireland sent thousands of Irish to Boston, and thousands settled in the milling communities of Lowell, Lawrence, and Fall River. Twentieth-century immigrants have come principally from Canada and the Maritime Provinces, Poland, Italy, Finland, and Germany. Today, only 40 per cent of the region's population can claim native parentage. Another 40 per cent were born here of mixed or foreign parentage. About one fifth of the people were born in other countries.[9]

New England's population is predominantly urban. In the nine metropolitan districts of New England, as delineated by the United States Census, five and a half million people are now living. The states where these metropolitan districts are found are three of the four most densely populated states of the nation. They are Massachusetts, Rhode Island, and Connecticut. Seventy-seven per cent of New England's population lives in towns and cities of more than twenty-five thousand people. In the past thirty years the urban areas have had consistent gains in population, whereas the rural areas have declined. The rural population is found in the minute lowlands, on the slopes of the uplands, and in the larger river valleys. It is a peculiar characteristic of southern New England that

---
[8] J. T. Adams, *New England in the Republic* (Boston: Little, Brown & Co., 1926), p. 150.
[9] *Statistical Abstract of The United States* (Washington: U. S. Government Printing Office, 1940); this is the source of all the statistics in this section.

one is never far from unsettled waste lands. Someone has remarked that the wilderness is just outside the metropolises of New England. The true and extensive wilderness area of New England, however, is to be found in northwestern Maine and the White Mountain area of New Hampshire. In these areas the density of population is less than two persons per square mile, whereas the density of southern New England is more than five hundred persons per square mile. The average density for the entire region is about one hundred thirty persons per square mile. Of course the southern metropolitan areas make the regional average high. Somerville, a city contiguous to Boston, has one hundred thousand people living in an area of less than four square miles.

From 1920 to 1940 the birth rate of New England fell from 23.6 per thousand to 15.1 per thousand. The net natural increase per thousand population for the United States is 6.1, but in New England it is only 3.4. This is typical of urban-metropolitan populations in the United States. It is noteworthy that recent population studies indicate that significant increases in the birth rate and in the net natural increase per thousand population will be in the rural, not the urban, centers of the United States. The New England Regional Planning Commission, the regional office of the National Resources Planning Board, estimates that the population of New England will remain relatively stable, with slow, consistent increases until a maximum of approximately nine million people inhabit the region. That few people have migrated to or from the region in the past decade or two indicates a certain stability in the population.

The cultural heritage of New England is exceedingly complex, but perhaps its very complexity adds to its richness. Until well into the middle of the nineteenth century, New England was economically, politically, and psychologically a well-knit region in which the people were almost homogeneous in race and religion. It was during this period that many of the great colleges were founded, that New England states took the lead in the nation in establishing free public schools, that the Anglo-Puritan stock established its leadership in literature, religion, and politics. But with the coming of age of newer industrial regions in the Middle West and the immigration of thousands of new peoples, in the latter half of the nineteenth century, New England faced not only economic competition but a real cultural transformation in its people.

The impact of the new peoples was felt in religion, for with the beginning of the twentieth century Roman Catholicism, the church of the Irish, French-Canadians, and Italians, became one of the dominant religions in the region. Now every city has its cathedrals and parochial schools, and the region has some of the largest Roman Catholic colleges. The impact of the new peoples has been manifested in politics. After being the Republican stronghold of the nineteenth century, New England, with the exception of the northern portions, is virtually Democratic today. Most of the newer peoples are Democrats. Several cities have areas which vote consistently for Democratic candidates. But there are some Republican strongholds also. The social structure of the metropolitan areas is determined somewhat by national origins. The Irish, Italians, Jews, Negroes, native stocks — each group seeks an area of the city in which to live and make their homes. There are schools in the Boston metropolitan area in which each of these national or racial groups finds an overwhelming majority. The writer has visited schools in one city where more than three-fourths of the children in one school are Jewish. Settlement houses take on racial and national characteristics also in the metropolitan areas. The names of political candidates must, in some areas, be of the same national flavor as the people who live there. The Boston *Herald*, commenting on the 1942 senatorial and gubernatorial elections, in which two Republicans were reëlected in Massachusetts, suggested that the reason for Democratic losses was that there were too few Irish names on the ballot. The power of the Roman Catholic Church was indicated in the same election when an amendment to the state constitution of Massachusetts permitting doctors to give advice on the control of births was defeated. The Church had campaigned vigorously against the amendment.

The significance of this racial and national mixture in New England is readily apparent to one who comes from another region. On every hand there is evidence of considerable intolerance. This has been the subject of discussion by leaders throughout the region, but there is little evidence to show that the problem is being solved. Students in training to be teachers have told the writer that because they are of a given religious group there is little hope of their obtaining a position in some cities. Some of these students were Jewish, some Irish, some Anglo-Protestant.

Certainly New England is cosmopolitan and heterogeneous today in race, religion, politics, and general culture. Throughout the region these newer peoples are developing leaders. Along with the Cabots, Lodges, Adamses, and Lowells, there have arisen the Cohens, Kellys, Murphys, LeBlancs, and others.

Nevertheless, of the entire nation, no region can boast of such diverse and valuable aesthetic resources. The Boston Symphony Orchestra, the Boston Museum of Fine Arts, the Harvard and Yale libraries, the stately architecture, the historical shrines, the little theaters, all are parts of the present New England culture. It must be recognized that most of these facets of culture — language, religion, arts, education — were introduced from Europe, and basically follow the pattern of western culture.

Economy

The manufacturing industries are the foundation of New England's economy. This is indicated by the fact that of the three and a half million wage earners in the region, 43 per cent are employed in the mechanical and manufacturing industries.

It is also attested by the fact that the value added by manufacturing in the region was two and a half billion dollars in 1938, or more than ten times the value of the region's farm products for that year. Accurate statistics on value added by manufactures during World War II are not yet available but it is estimated that the total is greater than five billion dollars. Furthermore, New England, with 2 per cent of the land area and 7 per cent of the national population, annually produces about 10 per cent of the total value of manufactured goods of the nation.

The manufacturing industries of New England are located almost entirely in Massachusetts, Connecticut, and Rhode Island. Yet there are important centers scattered throughout the region. The bulk of the manufacturing industries however, are concentrated in the metropolitan regions of southern New England.

Because New England is usually associated with textiles in the public mind, most people think the textile industry is the

RELATIVE PRODUCTION VALUE AND EMPLOYMENT IN THE MAJOR INDUSTRIAL GROUPS OF NEW ENGLAND
A ten-year average from 1929 to 1938

	Per cent of total value added by manufactures	Per cent of total wage earners in manufactures
Metal goods and related industries	27.4	23.4
Textiles	21.9	31.3
Paper and printing	11.2	7.7
Leather and rubber	9.7	12.1
Foodstuffs	5.9	3.6
Unclassified	23.9	21.9
Total	100.0	100.0

principal manufacturing activity. However, the metal-goods industries hold the highest rank as measured in value, with textiles ranking second. These two lead the other classified groups in manufacturing as shown in the accompanying table.[10]

[10] *Regional Planning, Part III, New England*, p. 92.

According to the New England Council, there are five items of manufacture in which New England produces more than 50 per cent of the national total.[11] These are firearms, woolens, cotton goods, boots and shoes, and textile machinery. Moreover, New England produces more than one fourth of the national output of silverware and plateware, cutlery, jewelry, clocks, hats, hardware, needles and pins, and sporting goods. Other items of which New England produces more than one fifth of the national total are wire, paper, marble, slate, granite, tools, and men's and boys' clothing. These facts are evidence of the diversity and specialization of manufactures in New England. Moreover, the type of manufacturing which is carried on in New England is one which requires skilled labor, considerable capital outlay, and a variety of raw materials.

The size of manufacturing establishments in New England is markedly different from that in other specialized manufacturing regions. Of the 14,000 establishments, 80 per cent employ 50 workers or less, and fewer than 3 per cent employ 500 workers or more. The larger mills are the textile plants, leather plants, shoe plants, firearms plants, and metal-goods mills.

Five important factors have aided New England in overcoming shortages of important raw materials for its industries. (1) Capital resources were available in New England during the early period of industrialization. (2) Water power from many coastal streams took the place of coal in many instances. (3) A continuous flow of low-cost labor from Europe helped young industries during the nineteenth century. (4) New England benefited from an early start in many of her established industries. (5) The region was accessible by sea to coastal markets and had the advantage of cheap transportation of bulky raw materials by sea.

The past fifty years have witnessed the continuous growth of New England industry as a whole, but the depression decade was a period of contraction of output. This situation was

[11] *New England's Record* (pamphlet; Boston: New England Council, 1939).

common to the entire nation, however, and in New England it was only in the cotton textiles that there was a marked decrease through industrial migration. World War II has stimulated industries of all kinds in New England, especially the metal-goods and shipbuilding industries. Higher prices and increased demands have somewhat revived many small plants for the manufacture of military clothing and shoes. The costs involved in railroad transportation of raw materials would seem to indicate that some of the heavy industries of New England which flourished during the War years may decline once the period of high prices and government buying have passed. Moreover, shipyards on the West Coast and textile mills in the Southeast are certainly capable of producing at lower costs in normal times. It seems, therefore, that the hope of New England lies in using the resources that are at hand, and in producing goods which require small transportation costs.

During the seventeenth and eighteenth centuries, New England's agriculture was developed as a form of self-sufficient domestic economy. Some products, such as cheese, meats, and lumber, were sold for city consumption and for export, but local and family self-sufficiency was the rule throughout the region. With the rise of industry in the nineteenth century, however, and the opening of the West, New England agriculture underwent considerable change. There was migration to the cities for industrial work, and the competition of western meat, grain, and other products from cheaper lands forced New England farmers to specialize in a few outstanding crops. I. G. Davis, of the Connecticut Agricultural College, has summarized the results of this transition period of the late nineteenth century in the following manner:

> By the beginning of the World War, New England agriculture had adjusted itself to the economic situation. The specialized production of potatoes in Aroostook County in Maine; of tobacco and onions in the Connecticut Valley; of cranberries in Plymouth and Barnstable counties in Massachusetts; of butter and maple syrup in Vermont; of

THE NEW ENGLAND REGION

blueberries along the coast of Washington County in Maine; and vegetable production near all population centers had appeared. The agriculture of the inland and upland regions, which constitute by far the greater part of New England, had become a form of general farming. Its core was dairying, around which were grouped minor enterprises in fruit, vegetable, and poultry production and usually the sale of forest products.[12]

Figure 15 shows the major kinds of farming areas of New England. It will be seen that few changes have taken place since World War I. The general farming areas usually produce dairy products, potatoes, truck vegetables, some fruits, and poultry. The fruit and berry areas vary somewhat: those on the uplands usually specialize in apples and those on Cape Cod produce cranberries, whereas the Maine berry areas are famous for blueberries. The non-agricultural areas, it will be noted, are chiefly located in the White Mountains and in the Maine wilderness. The semi-agricultural areas are the transition zones between non-agricultural areas and the general farming areas. Here an increasing number of summer resorts, hunting and fishing, and camping, are linked with lumbering and dairying and general farming. The tobacco areas are concentrated in Connecticut. With this tobacco-growing is some vegetable trucking on soils that will not produce the high-grade cigar-wrapper tobacco. Small dairies dot this region and all southern New England. Most of these dairy areas sell directly to consumers in urban centers. Intensive dairying is associated with the Champlain Valley in Vermont and the upper Connecticut Valley. Here, most of the land in farms is in pasture and hay and forests. The milk and dairy produce is shipped to large cities like Boston, Hartford, and New York. One of the most specialized agricultural areas is the potato area of Aroostook County in Maine. This is almost a one-crop region. There are small dairies in the area, however, and some general farming is associated with the commercial production of potatoes.

[12] *New England's Prospect: 1933*, p. 138.

Of New England's forty million acres, only five million are in field crops, while another five million are in pasture and hay. The rest of the area is made up of forests and cut-over or

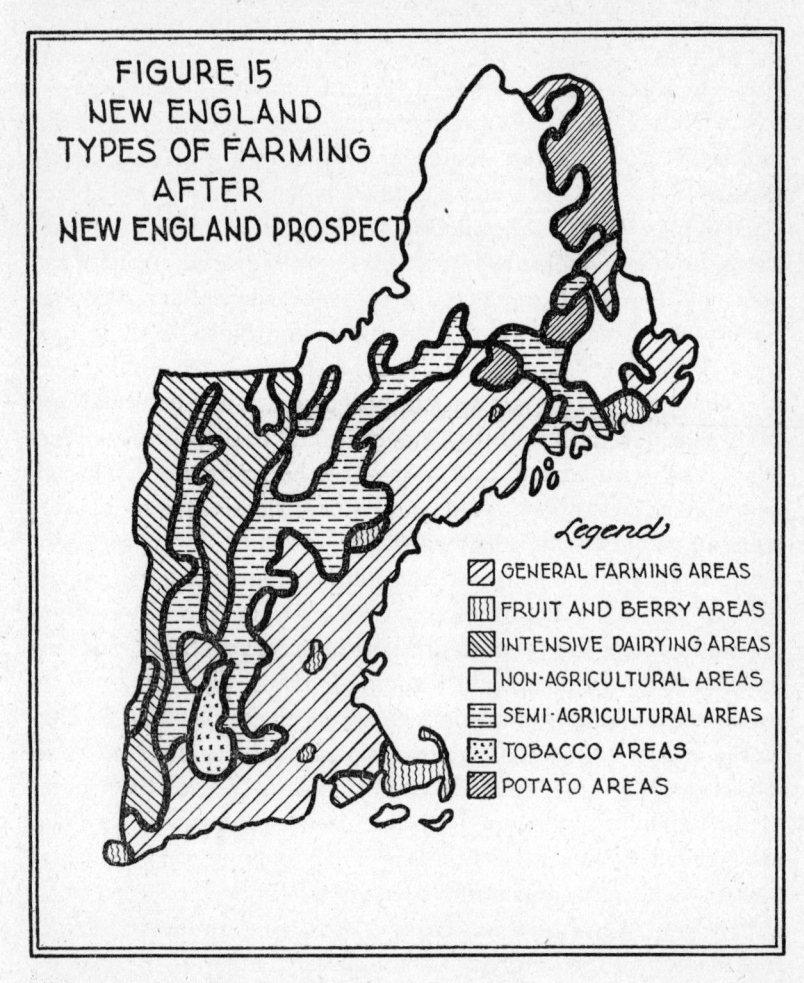

FIGURE 15
NEW ENGLAND
TYPES OF FARMING
AFTER
NEW ENGLAND PROSPECT

Legend
- GENERAL FARMING AREAS
- FRUIT AND BERRY AREAS
- INTENSIVE DAIRYING AREAS
- NON-AGRICULTURAL AREAS
- SEMI-AGRICULTURAL AREAS
- TOBACCO AREAS
- POTATO AREAS

abandoned farms. About half of Maine is wilderness, and throughout the region there are blocks of wastelands and unused acres. Nearly every farm has some woodland on it.

A significant development in New England has been the rise

of part-time farming. Thousands of people living close to some small mill or manufacturing plant earn part of their living by farming and part by working in the mill. Generally these part-time farmers raise vegetables and fruits, keep a cow, and raise some poultry. It has been a good thing for thousands, because the dual source of income is a type of insurance in depression years. It helps manufactures expand when possible, and it assures the worker of a source of income when manufactures decline.

A region so diverse as New England relies upon more than manufacturing and agriculture for its well-being. Among the other factors contributing to the regional economy are the fishing industry, finance and commerce, lumbering, recreational industries, and educational institutions.

The New England Council and the National Resources Planning Board estimate that in an ordinary year about one half billion dollars are spent in New England for recreation by tourists from outside and by people within the region. This expenditure covers railroad fares, gasoline purchases, resort rentals, auto supplies, and food. Within the past thirty years there has been a considerable movement of metropolitan populations from other regions to summer residences in the New England uplands and coastal areas. This movement has followed the abandonment of farms, especially in Vermont and New Hampshire. There has been a large movement into Connecticut by New Yorkers seeking air and light. Furthermore, the recreation industry is closely related to farming. Many farmers do part-time work in the businesses supplementary to recreation and summer travel to augment their incomes.

The fishing industry of the coast and of the North Atlantic is one of the oldest industries of New England. At the present time about seventeen thousand persons are engaged in fishing, and their annual earnings average approximately thirty million dollars. Three types of fishing are carried on by New Englanders: ground fishing for fish which inhabit the bottom of the ocean — haddock, cod, hake, and pollock; surface fishing for fish which run in schools — mackerel and herring; and shore fishing for shellfish and some flounders. New England catches one fifth of the total value of the fish caught by American fisheries.

Some of the oldest fortunes and banks of the nation are located in New England. According to the New England Council, New England, with only 7 per cent of the national population, has 8 per cent of the national wealth, 11 per cent of the capital resources in banks, 8 per cent of the nation's life insurance in force, 18 per cent of the savings deposits in the United States.[13] The per capita savings of New England is about five hundred dollars, whereas the rest of the nation averages about one hundred seventy-five dollars. New England has always been a wealth-accumulating region, and therefore is a region of influence in the total national economy.

The New England Regional Planning Commission estimates that New England schools and colleges have an annual income of more than sixty million dollars from tuitions. More than one third of this income is derived from students attending New England institutions from other regions. The Boston metropolitan area has several universities and colleges, and old, established academies are scattered throughout the region. Education is a source of income for thousands of New Englanders.

In the realm of commerce, both foreign and domestic, New England is a leading American region. The value of imports recorded as entered through all New England ports averages about $220,000,000 or five times the value of exports, while the volume is approximately five and a half million tons, or sixteen times the export tonnage.[14] Nearly all of New England's exports move through the port of New York. On the other hand, the imports of New England, especially the heavy, bulky products

---

[13] *New England's Record.*
[14] *Foreign Commerce Yearbook* (Washington: U. S. Department of Commerce, 1938).

such as crude petroleum and coal, move into New England through New England ports. The exports are light, expensive, finished materials. This creates a considerable shipping problem, for many ships must leave New England only partially filled. The two principal routes of railroad transportation of New England connect Boston with Albany and Boston with New York City. To the north of Boston another major route runs to Bangor, Maine; and in central New England, the Connecticut Valley is the route of much north–south traffic by rail.

This summary is by no means a complete picture of the regional economy of New England, but it does emphasize the salient features of the economy, and it indicates the diversity and stability of the region as a whole. There are many close relationships between the different facets of the economy, and there is an almost inextricable relation between the New England culture on the one hand and the regional economy on the other. It is not by chance that the ivy grew luxuriantly on Yale and Harvard while the grime accumulated on industrial Cambridge and New Haven. And, as the economy has matured, the tenement districts of the metropolises have grown. New England has weathered many crises in her economic development, and her stability today is the result of this continuous adjustment.

Some Important Regional Problems

A regional problem is one that is significant and pertinent to the life of a whole region. It may be localized, but it must have implications for more people and communities than the local community in which it occurs. There are many social and economic problems in New England that overlap state lines and have implications for people everywhere in the region, for the region's permanent well-being. The following discussion will present some of the more important regional problems of New England.

Among the problems which emphasize the need of a regional

approach and a regional solution, none speak so strongly as do those which arise from the depletion of natural resources. Attention has already been called to the depletion of the forests of New England. Obviously, no single state can solve this problem by itself; the forests extend over the entire region, and the fires, hurricanes, forest pests, and other destructive agencies do not stop at state lines. Laws and restrictions concerning forest utilization should be as continuous as the forest is from one state to another.

The conservation of regional water resources also calls for a regional approach. Since most of the major streams of New England are interstate streams, attempts to enforce regulations dealing with stream pollution, the development of water power, the provisions for flood control and for recreational development, all call for regional planning. The uses to which the Connecticut River is put in Vermont or New Hampshire often affect its value in Connecticut and Massachusetts. The Merrimack, the Blackstone, and other rivers are examples of water resources calling for regional development.

One aspect of the fishing industry that has been discussed widely in recent years is the decline of the lobster industry. In 1889 about thirty million pounds of lobsters were caught off the New England shores. By 1939, the annual catch was about twelve million pounds. The simple fact is that more lobsters have been taken from the sea than nature can replace. Moreover, stream pollution has deposited poisonous refuse and noxious wastes from the mills and cities along the streams. This stifles the breeding centers for the lobsters. The lobster catch is drawn from nearly every state, and the problem even becomes international in its Canadian relationships.

The migratory character of game birds and waterfowl makes it imperative that there be some general regional approach to the problem of certain kinds of wild-life conservation. The fresh-water fish of the interstate streams should be conserved through regional action.

THE NEW ENGLAND REGION 61

There is a close relationship between the development of recreational industries and the conservation of natural resources. The recreational industries flourish where nature is kept alive and beautiful. Polluted streams, lakes and streams and forests without wild life, and unkempt wastelands are not attractive. They are simply evidences of man's disregard for nature.

Since streams, forests, wild life, and soils are all related and either thrive or perish together, it is difficult to see how an attack could be made upon the problem of total conservation without relating the group. There is need then to survey the present regional natural resources, and to plan for their conservation and development in terms of the needs of the people and the potentialities of the resources.

Basic to industry, agriculture, and other factors of New England life is the problem of transportation. Many of the present highways of New England are routed through congested areas where speed is lost and accident rates are high. Much of the agricultural produce and industrial goods is moved by truck to other regions and to metropolitan centers. Through ways are needed from farms to markets and for the development of the tourist industry. Certainly no single state could develop an adequate program of highway development today or in the future without close coöperation and planning with its neighboring states. Research is needed on the daily, weekly, and seasonal flow of traffic throughout the region before a highway system can be planned for the total well-being of the region.

The past decade has witnessed a phenomenal growth of air travel and transport, and it would seem that future developments in this field point toward enlarging facilities and replanning of routes in and through New England. This calls for regional planning of navigation aids, such as radio, direction beacons, light beacons, and weather stations. It means extending the present fields and the integration of the routes and systems of air transportation. The significance of air travel and transport is very pointed for New England, for nearly three fourths of the national population is within a few hours of New England. Moreover, New England is the northeastern end of the national airways today, and in the future it will probably be an important link in international airways to Europe and Canada. To attempt to plan for the future of the airways in terms of localities or states would seem rather ridiculous. National and international planning on a global scale will probably take place in terms of the major regions of the earth. New England's unique situation will probably make it a link in the routes which will encircle the globe after the war.

Railroad development in New England has come through the consolidation of many small lines. Competition with trucks and busses has placed many spurs out of business in recent years. One of the knottiest problems of the railroads is that more freight moves into the region than moves out of the region. This often means that empty cars have to be hauled back to the regions from which they started for new loads. Moreover, the setting of rates, the planning of recreational industries, and the problems involved in fitting railway transportation into the picture with the evolving airways and highways are problems which call for a regional attack. A small beginning has been made on regional integration of railways. There has been some regional planning in terms of rate-making and in planning for consolidation.

The ocean-going commerce of New England needs thorough study in relation to other types of transportation and in relation to the needs of the region and the regional ports. The great port of the region, Boston, has been in the process of decline for many years, and it is certainly not developed as a modern port. Other ports are important also, and there is needed some regional consideration of port developments. Some materials will probably continue to come into the region by water, but perhaps the development of air transport after the war will change the methods of export and import for some goods. Effective integration of the several types of transportation in New England must be accomplished in terms of the whole region, and in terms of all the people.

Many of the transportation and conservation problems overlap and interpenetrate several of the prominent industrial problems of New England. Thus it would be impossible to consider them separately except for purposes of discussion.

Finding markets for New England's products is one of the most important problems of the region. This does not mean that New England should attempt to prosper at the expense of other regions, but it should certainly attempt to distribute its products so that the regional population can have a relatively stable economic situation. This may mean the development of foreign markets, or it may mean the effective distribution of goods to other American regions. The New England Council has already attacked this problem by advertising, by research studies, and by regional meetings.

Competent observers suggest that there is a need to integrate the agricultural activities with the industrial activities of New England. Part-time farming has already developed within the region, but there is need to extend this activity, which is thought to offer a solution to seasonal unemployment. Further development of part-time farming would call for some overall planning and surveying in terms of industry and agriculture. It would be difficult for a single state to mesh seasonal slack in industry with seasonal needs on the farm.

The move towards decentralization in industry is one which calls for a regional understanding and a regional approach. Industries overlap state lines and often move across state lines, or the industry may be in one state and the workers may live in another. The adjustments of taxation, transportation, housing, and other factors to the movements and adjustments of various industries call for a larger sphere of action and planning than a single state possesses. Educational problems, such as the equalizing of opportunities for youth through federal grants-in-aid, the development of effective vocational training centers, the planning of adult-educational facilities, and the focusing of educational facilities upon the needs of human beings — all these call for a regional approach.

The decline of an industry or of agriculture in a given community is always accompanied by social maladjustment. Several studies which illustrate this phenomenon have been made in New England. Nute Ridge, a small community in southern New Hampshire, is an example of such a community.[15] First settled in 1800, the town soon became a thriving agricultural community and prospered for nearly fifty years. Then the town developed home shoe-making, and the farms were allowed to deteriorate. When shoe-making shifted to metropolitan centers, in the era following the Civil War, the town became virtually bankrupt. The population dwindled to about half its former number; young people went elsewhere; and the farms, which had been allowed to run down, were of little value. The town has never been able to come back and hold its place with other comparable towns. Deerfield, New Hampshire, is another community which failed to adjust to changing conditions.[16] Hundreds of examples of this type could be cited to show how social problems arise out of long-run economic shifts and trends of a region. The realistic community recognizes its role in the total regional and national setting and is aware of its problems in terms of the trends and future possibilities of the region. The decline of a community can seriously disrupt the schools, churches, and social organizations of all kinds. Too many New England communities have collapsed in the past because they failed to comprehend and adjust themselves to the changes of a regional nature outside the community.

The lack of adequate health facilities and doctors is a serious problem in some parts of New England. The Boston newspapers

[15] H. C. Woodworth, *Nute Ridge: The Problem of a Typical Back-Town Community* (Durham, N. H.: Univ. of New Hampshire Extension Circular 68, 1927).
[16] E. C. Cogswell, *History of Nottingham, Deerfield, and Northwood* (Manchester, N. H., 1878).

on occasion carry advertisements placed by small communities for doctors. While some parts of the region have an oversupply of doctors, the rural districts usually have a difficult time in keeping a doctor.

Social welfare workers have, for the most part, placed a disproportionate emphasis upon metropolitan problems. In New England there are few social service organizations, aside from the Grange, which take an interest in the problems of rural communities. Much emphasis is placed upon the metropolitan districts of southern New England. Almost all the data on social-welfare work in New England deal with Boston, Providence, New Haven, Hartford, and Fall River. In 1928, the Vermont Commission on Country Life was organized to survey the rural problems of that state. Its report, *Rural Vermont: A Program for the Future*, was published in 1931. The recommendations of this committee with respect to the social problems and social welfare of rural Vermont, may, to some extent, represent typical conditions for much of rural New England. Among other recommendations were the suggestions that the towns subsidize physicians and hire resident nurses, that an increased effort be made to immunize children against communicable diseases, and that local health and welfare officers secure more adequate training. The report advocated the abolition of state "poor farms" and the development of a systematic method of dealing with poor relief. This Vermont commission has pointed out some of the prominent types of social problem common to many rural areas in New England.

About one eighth of the rural farm population of New England is foreign born. The social problems of these people in various communities are many and complex. The intermingling of differing ethnic groups with varying cultural backgrounds of religion and language often produces social conflict. While these groups intermingle in an economic sense in the ordinary transactions in the market place, often the intermingling stops there. In a small community there may be two or three recent immigrant groups who are submerged socially and who play little or no role in the political or social life of the community. They may even retain their language for decades. Recent studies by J. L. Hypes [17] and A. E. Cance [18] point out these problems of acculturation and social conflict in rural New England. A community in which such problems exist ought to be brought to a larger conception of social life than the local community. That is, if the older inhabitants of the community, who are usually the oppressors in this conflict, could visualize this problem on a regional basis — as a problem which rose above the petty affairs and social life of a small town — they might be willing to produce programs of social education, social recreation, and adult education which would help to solve the problem. It is a national as well as a regional need.

These are but a few of the major social problems which take on a character that is distinctive to New England, and which are closely related to other regional problems in industry, conservation, transportation, and general regional well-being. They are problems which may find a particular locus, but they are also problems which have implications for the entire region.

RECENT TRENDS IN REGIONAL INTEGRATION AND COÖPERATION

Since the days when the colonists formed the New England Confederation to fight the Indian wars, through the stormy periods of the War of 1812 and the Civil War, there have been repeated instances of New Englanders' working and planning together for the solution of their common problems. In recent decades, groups from the several New England states have again joined together for making a regional attack on some of the major regional problems. The regional groups now existing are few, and each is organized for a specific purpose. Most of them are less than twenty years old. It is the purpose here to

[17] *Social Participation in a Rural New England Town* (New York: Teachers College, Columbia University, 1927).
[18] "Immigrant Rural Communities," in the *Country Life Annals*, vol. 40 (1912).

THE NEW ENGLAND REGION

outline and describe briefly these relatively recent movements which indicate the rising regional consciousness of community interests in New England.

The New England Council is the organization which represents industry and business in New England. It was created in 1925 through the joint coöperation of the six New England governors, and is composed of business leaders from each state. In its tenth year the Council published a report on its work entitled *New England Today*. This report indicated that the Council had organized a research bureau with headquarters in Boston, Massachusetts, and this bureau published reports and planned advertising campaigns for recreational and industrial developments in New England. According to one of its recent publications, *New England's Record*, a statistical summary of New England's industry, the New England Council

seeks to arouse public interest in and support for the improvement of New England's economic performance, to vitalize and integrate activities which will increase the prosperity of the people of New England, and to enlarge the field of coöperation of the six states with one another and with the business community.

While a group of this sort may be inclined to make a rather roseate self-appraisal, it must be said that the New England Council has carried on a tremendous advertising campaign for industry, recreation, and general regional development. During the past decade the New England recreational industry has risen from a rather low spot in the economic structure of the region to second place as a source of income. The Council serves as a regional chamber of commerce in New England.

Several local and state farm groups have organized themselves into a regional farm organization for the six New England states. The Agricultural Council of New England is a young organization, formed in 1942. The Agricultural Council represents about forty farm organizations. As yet no major statement of purpose or of work has been made by the organization. The impetus for the organization came from the attempts of

John L. Lewis to organize the farmers, especially the dairy farmers of Vermont, into a union as a branch of the Congress of Industrial Organizations.[19] This organization could certainly find some major goals and aims to strive for that would be above the fighting of the unionization of the dairy farmers. Certainly there are sufficient rural problems for such an organization to tackle.

The New England Regional Planning Commission is the regional office for the National Resources Planning Board. It is the major federal research agency for New England. Since its funds are derived from the national treasury, its policy is largely a federal policy. The research and technical staff of the Planning Commission is paid by the federal government. The six states, however, have some influence on the Commission, for each sends a delegate to the board of directors. One of the major tasks of the Commission is to conduct research and prepare surveys on needed public-works programs. It also carries on investigations prior to the erection of federal buildings and the investment of federal moneys in real estate in New England. The purposes of the Commission were stated in its first publication, *Regional Planning, Part III, New England*. The introduction to the monograph states that the

concept of the meeting which organized the Commission was that the Commission should — 1. Be non partisan. 2. Have a representative from each State Planning Board. 3. Be permanent and provide for continuous review and revision of its plans. 4. Have a program of activities comprehensive in scope. 5. Concern itself with physical planning and study social and economic factors to determine their relation to and effect on physical plans. 6. Provide opportunity for local interest and civic organizations to forming a New England plan. 7. Be an organization separate and apart from administrative and construction agencies. 8. Coordinate state plans.

The Commission has made several studies of New England's problems such as agriculture, transportation, population trends,

[19] *Christian Science Monitor*, July 18, 1942.

natural resources, river and water problems, community planning, and industrial problems. The reports of the Commission are used in most universities and colleges as primary source materials, and many public schools make use of their bulletins. The Commission hopes to produce a basic regional plan for New England that will help all the agencies and all the people in the region to work together for the common welfare.

A factor of considerable significance in integrating a region, already mentioned in Chapter II, is the administrative process of the federal government. Within the past twenty years the federal government has assumed an increasingly important role in the lives of most people. The income tax, programs of social security, of public works, of conservation, and of health and education, all are important ways in which the federal government reaches into the lives of all citizens. In order to facilitate the administration of these and other programs, the federal government has established through its bureaus and departments many regional offices. Today almost every large city has an imposing Federal Building which houses these offices. New England is one of these administrative regions for many bureaus and departments. It has been the regional administrative district for the War Production Board, the Office of Price Administration, the National Youth Administration, the United States Army, the Office of Civilian Defense, and for many other important national governmental departments. The establishment of regional offices by the federal government is an attempt to take into account the variety of the American scene, to fit all the regions into the national scene more effectively by having a local office in each. These regional offices in New England center many of New England's problems and give New England an interest in the functioning of the large and complex national government of the United States.

Educational organizations have been flourishing in New England on a regional basis for many years. Prominent in the list of such organizations are the New England Association for

Colleges and Secondary Schools, the New England Mathematics Association, the New England Association for English Teachers, the New England Vocational Guidance Association, and the New England Council for the Social Studies. The basis for each organization is apparent in the name. One of the organizations has stated its aims very effectively to show its promise in regional development. This organization, the New England Council for the Social Studies, organized in 1941, states its goals in the following manner:

To provide for the study, discussion and distribution of ideas relative to better teaching of the social studies.

To provide a clearing house of information for the maintenance of desirable public relations.

To sponsor the publication of desirable articles, reports, and surveys of value to New England social studies teachers.

To promote the formation of regional and local discussion groups where more intimate discussion of problems of local interest may be considered.

To help coördinate the many worthwhile activities of existing organizations and make their efforts more widely known.[20]

The Council publishes a mimeographed bulletin which carries ideas and information to the members. Two meetings are held each year, and usually one meeting is devoted to a discussion of New England's problems.

National businesses have made New England a regional unit for administrative purposes also. Among these are the Atlantic and Pacific Tea Company, Sears Roebuck, the American Telephone and Telegraph Company, and several other firms. These businesses recognize New England as a distinct unit in the nation and they adjust their sales campaigns, their stocks of merchandise, and their plans of operation to the regional character. More than one hundred and fifty firms begin their firm names in the region with "New England." The region has its own radio network — the Yankee Network. The large Boston

[20] *New England Councilor*, vol. I, no. 1, p. 6.

THE NEW ENGLAND REGION

newspapers, such as the *Traveler*, the *Post*, the *Herald*, the *Globe*, and the *Christian Science Monitor*, are all read regionally. Each carries New England news. A singular incidence which indicates the regional character of these papers is that whenever war casualty lists were given out they were listed as casualties for New England, and later by states and cities.

Certain major events in the sports world are regional in character, such as the Rockingham, Suffolk, and Narragansett racing seasons, the skiing season, the summer-camp season, the football season for secondary schools, and the hunting seasons.

All of these factors combine to help integrate and coördinate the region. They help make the people of New England conscious of the fact that they are New Englanders. They have resulted from the needs of the people, and they thrive because they satisfy certain demands for organizations and for teamwork on a regional basis. Not all of these organizations are thriving as they would like to or as they should. Further development is needed in all of them. Moreover, all of these organizations need to know more about each other. They need to work together more, and perhaps some of them need to combine their efforts.

Summary

New England may be considered a region in a historical, a geographical, an economic, and a sociological sense. The resources of New England are not rich, but they are of the type which, with careful husbanding, remains valuable for centuries. The population of the region has been derived from many sources, and is largely urban in character. The economy of New England is stable, diverse, and traditional. Manufacturing, commerce, finance, recreation, and agriculture are the main features of the regional economy. Many problems of New England are compelling people to view the region as a whole in seeking solutions. The problems of most significance are those arising from industry, from the land, and from the social matrix.

New England has a long history of regional coöperation and integration, and recent trends indicate that coöperation is again an important factor in the solution of regional problems. There is need, however, for the various regional agencies to work together more closely for the well-being of the entire region.

CHAPTER IV

THE STUDY OF NEW ENGLAND REGIONAL LIFE IN NEW ENGLAND SCHOOLS

IN AN ATTEMPT to determine how fully the social-studies programs of New England schools are informing youth about the life and problems of New England, a cursory examination was made, through visits and communication with teachers of a small group of programs. This survey indicated that little or no emphasis had been placed upon the study of the economy, resources, problems, or recent social trends of New England. A more objective and more wide-spread survey was then made to test this tentative conclusion.

Four sources of information were used: (1) supervisors of elementary and secondary education in each of the State Departments of Education of the six New England States; (2) a group of educational leaders familiar with the social studies curriculums of New England schools; (3) the most widely used social-studies textbooks in New England schools; and (4) the teachers of the social studies in New England.

THE OPINIONS OF STATE SUPERVISORS

Every New England state has a department of education. In some departments there are several supervisors, whereas in others there are only two or three. For the purposes of this study, inquiries were sent to each state supervisor of secondary schools and to each state supervisor of rural or elementary education. Rhode Island has no supervisors of general secondary or elementary education, so the State Director of Education was asked to recommend a leader in each field to speak for the state. The complete list of supervisors with their correct titles and addresses appears in Appendix B.

To ascertain what New England schools are teaching New England youth about the life and problems of New England, the following questions were addressed to each state supervisor:

Do you know of any curriculum revision programs now in progress in the elementary or secondary schools of [the state] which are aimed at acquainting youth with the resources, economy, problems, and recent social trends of New England as a region?

Do you know of any outstanding courses or units now being taught either in the elementary or secondary schools of [the state] which are aimed at the same objectives as those stated in question one?

The complete letter is in Appendix A.

All the answers to the first question were negative. That is, there are no major curriculum-revision programs now in progress in elementary or secondary schools aimed at acquainting New England youth with the economy, resources, problems, and recent social trends of New England. Several of the supervisors mentioned local curriculum-revision programs in terms of local or community or state life and problems, but none knew of any programs aimed at presenting New England youth with a knowledge of New England life and problems. Curriculum revision on the high-school level in the social studies is now being planned in Vermont through a state committee, and in the elementary schools in New Hampshire by a state committee.

In answering the second question, the state supervisors, with the exception of two, knew of no outstanding units or courses now being taught which are aimed at acquainting New England youth with the resources, economy, problems, and recent social trends of New England. In a group of rural schools in Connecticut, a fifth-grade unit on New England is taught. The unit covers many facets of New England life — history, geography, industries, social life. So many topics are treated in a few weeks by elementary school children that little depth can be reached. In New Hampshire, pupils enrolled in commercial geography courses on the high-school level study a series of units on the geography of New England if the local

THE NEW ENGLAND SCHOOLS 75

school follows the State Course of Study. It is not mandatory that schools follow the State Course of Study, and there is no state adoption of textbooks, hence the appearance of the units in the state guide is not evidence that such units are widely taught. Moreover, only a small percentage of high-school pupils study commercial geography. No high-school or junior-high-school courses dealing with New England were reported.

The state supervisors are in a position to know what is being done in their individual states: it would seem from their reports that no major curriculum-revision programs are now in progress in the social studies generally in New England, and that little or no emphasis is placed upon the study of New England regional life.

The Opinions of Social-Studies Leaders

To secure information on the same questions that were sent to the state supervisors, a group of prominent educators in New England who are intimately associated with the social-studies programs was selected. Of the eighteen who made up the group, half were college teachers who had had a long experience in teacher training in New England; four were city supervisors of the social studies in large New England cities; one was a prominent high-school teacher of the social studies; two were high-school principals who had previously shown leadership in the social studies; one was a superintendent of schools who had had experience in curriculum reorganization in the social studies; and one was a dean of a college of education. The geographical location by states was the following: Maine two; Vermont one; Massachusetts seven; New Hampshire two; Connecticut five; and Rhode Island one. Thus each state was represented. Furthermore, the major colleges and universities contributed a member of the group. The complete list of leaders is in Appendix C.

Two educators reported specific curriculum-revision projects on the high-school level which were aimed at teaching the life and problems of New England to New England youth. At Hingham, Massachusetts, the ninth-grade course in Civics has recently been revised to include a group of units on New England life. The first half year of the course is devoted to a study of Hingham, and the second half year centers on New England. There are units on New England which deal with the resources, problems, culture, and problems of regional planning. Each unit is studied about four weeks. In the schools of Brookline, Massachusetts, a half course dealing with New England life and problems is now being planned for the junior year in high school. The course will be elective and will consist of a series of five units somewhat similar to the Hingham high-school course on the ninth-grade level. The Brookline high-school course on New England was still in the planning stage (January, 1943), but the Hingham course was already being taught.

No other educational leader reported curriculum-revision programs to teach the life and problems of New England to New England youth.

In answer to the second question on outstanding courses or units now being taught, the leaders generally knew nothing to report. Several reported outstanding programs of community study, but only one reported outstanding studies of New England life or problems. Several leaders mentioned that the study of New England was incidental in the regular courses which dealt with American life. Most of the leaders asked for information from the writer on what to teach or what other schools were doing. According to these leaders, who should have wide knowledge of what is taught in New England schools, little or no emphasis is placed upon the study of the life and problems of New England as a region.

AN ANALYSIS OF WIDELY USED SOCIAL-STUDIES TEXTBOOKS

It is the opinion of most social-studies specialists that the textbook is still the principal determinant of what is taught in the social studies. It was thought, therefore, that one of the best ways to determine what is being done in New England schools to acquaint youth with the life and problems of the region would be to examine the leading social-studies textbooks used throughout the region today. While it would be almost impossible to discover just how the books are used in all communities, or what books were used by each community, certainly such a survey would reveal the broad outline of content of the social studies in the region. Moreover, when it is revealed that two or three American history textbooks for the senior high school are used by nearly all the schools in the region, one may conclude that the content of such history courses, no matter where taught, is somewhat similarly conceived. The differences in the courses are apt to be the same as the differences in the textbooks used. It is recognized, however, that such a survey has limitations in that exact, quantitative statements on just how many schools are teaching an idea cannot be given. But from the survey one may conclude generally what the schools are teaching, and one may estimate the possibilities of teaching the life and problems of New England from the various books used. Thus, if a book which deals in no way with New England life is widely used in the eighth grade, one might conclude that little emphasis is placed upon the study of New England according to the textbook most widely used.

With several hundred textbooks from which to choose, a problem of no small importance was that of selecting the books that were widely used in New England. The term "widely used" means that a book is used by about one fourth of the schools. Since no study of this kind has been made except by publishers, the writer consulted a large publishing house. Publishers through their salesmen and agents made periodic surveys of textbooks. The publishing house consulted is one of the largest school-book publishing companies in America. Moreover, the writer had some knowledge of books used in several cities — the bulk of the school children of New England are in large cities, and through private conferences with teachers and supervisors a list was created. Professor Howard E. Wilson, a prominent leader in the social studies, also advised on selections. By several means a list was created which it was thought was inclusive enough to contain the names of the widely used textbooks in the social-studies programs of New England schools.

For purposes of classification for discussion the books were grouped in the following manner: (1) Elementary School: Geography, History, and Civics and Fusion; (2) Junior High School: Geography, History, and Civics and Fusion; (3) Senior High School: Geography, American History, Sociology, Problems of Democracy, and Economics.[1] World History, European History, and Ancient History were excluded because it was thought that very little would be included there on New England life.

The textbooks analyzed in this study that are widely used in the elementary schools are for the fourth, fifth, and sixth grades only, because there are relatively few books which present systematic studies of American life for the primary grades. In most schools organized instruction in the social studies does not appear until the fourth grade. Two principal studies constitute the social studies in most schools, geography and history. There are some schools which use integrated or fused textbooks, namely those books which are organized in units in which geography, civics, and history are combined, or in which the geography, history, and civics are taught in alternate units as one continuous program or curriculum.

The thirteen history books most widely used in New Eng-

---

[1] This pattern of organization was taken from the *Bibliography of Textbooks in The Social Studies*, Bulletin No. 12 of the National Council for the Social Studies (Washington, D. C., 1939). This bibliography is the most comprehensive listing in existence of social-studies textbooks.

THE NEW ENGLAND SCHOOLS 79

land's elementary schools were written as five series by five different groups of authors and published by five different publishers. The series are somewhat alike in that each covers the history of the United States (usually in two books), and the European backgrounds of America (usually in one book). The complete list of all textbooks considered is to be found in Appendix D. If the content of these books is indicative of what is commonly taught in New England schools about New England life, it would seem that the treatment and study are very sketchy and vague. Not only are a great many topics treated, but the treatment is very general and the discussion on any one topic is brief. Under colonial life most of the histories for elementary schools dwell briefly on New England. The typical topics are "England Colonizes America"; "The Pilgrims Come to the New World"; "The Founding of New England"; and "Life in Old New England." Usually one of these topics has about three or four pages of discussion. In no widely used elementary history book did the writer find a whole unit or group of chapters devoted to the colonial history of New England. Moreover, in no textbook did the writer find any discussion of New England life in the nineteenth or twentieth century. Evidently the writers of these history books have tried to include some of everything that has happened in American history with little or no emphasis upon any particular state or region. New England schools use books that are widely used throughout the United States, and thus there is little emphasis upon New England. Most of the topics which deal with New England are so broad and general that it is almost impossible for the textbooks to give much detail or specific information and discussion. The general conclusion which the writer came to after reading the set of history books was that in most elementary schools in New England the colonial history of the region is studied in the fifth or sixth grade, depending upon the textbook series used. There is no further study of the development of New England beyond the colonial stage except for incidental references to the region as the home of Webster, Whittier, or other great men.

As with the history books, the most widely used geography textbooks in the elementary schools of New England appear in series. Three of these series are widely used throughout the region: the Atwood-Thomas Series, the McConnell Series, and the Stull and Hatch Series. Each of these series has one book on the geography of the United States or of North America. Each presents one chapter or one unit on the New England States. Usually this study comes in the fifth grade and ordinarily requires about three or four weeks, depending upon the school. The topics treated are practically the same in all the books. They are farming in New England; the fishing industry in New England; the manufacturing industries of New England; seaports and cities of New England; the climate of New England; and other like topics. Usually each book devotes about twenty to thirty pages to the discussion of New England. About half of these pages are filled with illustrations, so that the treatment is quite general. For example, one book treats the cities of New England in less than four hundred words. One point should be made here for the geographies: some discussion is made of life in the twentieth century.

The three fusion series which are widely used in the elementary schools of New England are Wilson, Wilson, and Erb; Rugg and Krueger; and Bruner and Smith. None of these books treat New England as a region. The units are organized and presented for national use, and they would have to be supplemented in nearly every region or community with other books if an adequate treatment were given to community or regional study.

From the survey of the most widely used elementary-school social-studies textbooks in New England schools, it is possible to draw the following conclusions:

(1) The history books for the intermediate elementary

THE NEW ENGLAND SCHOOLS 81

grades usually include a discussion of the founding of the New England colonies. They do not include a discussion of life in the nineteenth or twentieth century.

(2) The geography books present a survey of New England as a region in which as many as ten or thirteen topics are discussed in a general manner.

(3) The fusion textbooks do not treat New England as a region.

On the junior-high-school level the most widely used textbooks are also organized in series, and the series are widely used. This is true for histories, geographies, and fusion courses. The civics books are generally singly issued.

The history textbooks treat the history of the United States in somewhat the same fashion as the elementary history books do, with a wide variety of topics and a large amount of general discussion. There is the usual short discussion of the colonization and settlement of New England, and then the region is studied only incidentally during the nineteenth and twentieth centuries. One book devotes a single paragraph to the discussion of the textile industry in New England in the late nineteenth century. Another presents scattered sentences on industrial and social life in New England during the nineteenth century. There is some treatment of sectionalism and the Civil War as a result of sectionalism and disunity among the parts of the nation. There is no discussion of the meaning of the diversity of natural resources in the nation, or of the regional configuration of American life.

The geography books which are widely used in the junior high schools of New England are chiefly topical. That is, the approach is through products or economic activities and not through regions. It is difficult to find regional discussions of agriculture, manufacturing, or commerce; and, where they do exist, they exist as scattered sentences in the geography books. There are some geographies which treat New England as a region for junior high school pupils and there are special supplements on New England, but they are certainly not widely used in New England schools.

The fusion books of Rugg are widely used in New England by many school systems. They deserve special mention therefore. There are references to New England life scattered through the books which deal with America, and one text contains a brief study of American Regions, but the study is but one unit.

The ninth-grade civics books which are widely used in New England place most of their emphasis upon national government. They do not place emphasis upon any particular region, nor do they emphasize the regional administration of law by the federal government. They do not discuss interstate coöperation and planning. Such topics if discussed properly would be helpful in regional study, but they are not covered in the ninth-grade texts in New England schools.

The conclusion which was reached after studying the most widely used social-studies books in the junior high schools of New England was that little or no emphasis was placed upon the study of New England as a region.

On the senior high-school level the widely used textbooks are national in character and discussion. That is, they, like the textbooks for the elementary schools and the junior high schools, are written for national use. None of the books which are widely used in New England place emphasis upon the regional nature of American life or upon the regional character of American problems. New England is mentioned in some of the books, but only in an incidental manner. There is treatment of sectionalism and its evils in the history books, but there is no discussion of the recent regional movement towards interstate coöperation. The economics books still deal largely with the classical frame of reference — production, distribution, consumption, and exchange. The sociology books are largely

THE NEW ENGLAND SCHOOLS 83

studies of social institutions and social problems. The problems-of-democracy books are replete with national problems, but there is little or no attempt to give these problems a setting or a cultural background in terms of the regional nature of American life. Geography is not widely studied by pupils in New England high schools. Those books that do treat New England do it only incidentally. Most of them are topical geographies, and most are economic geographies. A typical reference to New England in an index of one of the social-studies books would be something like this:

New England, 68, 104, 286.

There would appear on the pages named about two sentences, in which mention would be made of colonization, the decline of textiles, or the industries of the region. There is no general treatment of New England in the high-school social-studies textbooks which are widely used in New England. There are many scattered references to the region running through the history, geography, and problems-of-democracy textbooks. While some textbooks do take the factor of the regional nature of American life into account, the writer believes that none of these books are widely used in New England. Certainly there is no evidence to support the idea that textbooks are selected for New England high schools because they present clear, realistic, and interesting portrayals of New England life.

The general conclusion to the textbook survey must be that in New England schools the textbooks most widely used do not place emphasis upon the regional nature of American life nor upon the characteristics of the resources, economy, problems, and recent social trends of New England. A youth in any other American region receives about the same information on New England as a New England youth, judging solely by the textbooks used in the schools. Certainly many of the textbooks that are widely used in New England are very popular in other regions. One point should be added here with respect to teaching materials: the New England Regional Planning Commission has produced many surveys and reports on New England which are used in a few schools, but according to the authorities at the Planning Commission there is no widespread use of their materials by the public schools in New England. Certainly the bulk the schools make no use whatever of the materials.

WHAT THE TEACHERS SAY

To discover what teachers were teaching youth in New England about its region, a questionnaire was devised for a selected group of teachers to check. The questionnaire was made after a study of New England, from recent regional surveys, and from what the writer thought might feasibly be taught about New England in the social-studies programs. Topics covering a wide range were listed so that the questionnaire would allow the teacher considerable freedom, and space was left at the bottom for the inclusion of topics not listed. The teachers were asked to list the teaching aids and materials — books, collateral readings, maps, moving pictures, etc. — which they found valuable in teaching the life and problems of New England. The questionnaire and the letter which was sent with it are found on the following pages. They are included here to help the reader understand the findings and conclusions reached.

HARVARD UNIVERSITY
GRADUATE SCHOOL OF EDUCATION

Lawrence Hall, Kirkland Street   Cambridge, Massachusetts

The writer is undertaking a study of materials and plans for adjusting the social studies programs of New England schools to the life and problems of New England. An important part of the study deals with the present treatment of New England as a region in the social studies programs. To discover what the schools are now doing, a selected group of specialists, teachers, and administrators are being asked to help the writer.

Three problems constitute the basis of this request: 1. What units

THE NEW ENGLAND SCHOOLS

or topics are taught in New England schools which deal with the life and problems of New England? 2. At what grade levels, or, in what courses and subjects are such topics and units taught? and, 3. What teaching materials — textbooks, films, collateral readings, maps, etc. — have proved most valuable in teaching the factors of New England's life and problems?

The enclosed questionnaire lists topics on the geography, population, historical background, economy, and problems of New England. You are asked to place an X in one of the two columns opposite each topic. If you spend less than two weeks on a given topic, place an X in the column under *Little or No Emphasis*. If you teach a unit on the topic or spend at least two or more weeks on the topic, place an X under *Much Emphasis*. If you treat several of the topics under a major heading, you may indicate this by enclosing these topics in a bracket. Be sure that you indicate at the top of the questionnaire the grade level or subject course in which you teach the topics you check. There is a place at the bottom of the questionnaire for additional topics which are not listed on the questionnaire.

On the back of the questionnaire will you please list the materials — textbooks, films, collateral readings, maps, etc. — which you have found very valuable in teaching the life and problems of New England.

The study is being made under the direction of Professor Howard E. Wilson of Harvard University. If you return the questionnaire, the results of the study will be made available to you. A stamped and addressed envelope is enclosed for your return of the questionnaire. May I have your help?

Sincerely yours,
Royce H. Knapp

Name_____ School_____

Grade_____ Subject_____

Little or No Emphasis	Much Emphasis	*An Outline of Topics of the New England Region*
		I. Geography and Natural Resources
		Topography
		Climate
		Soils

Forest Resources
Water Resources — The Ocean
Wildlife Resources

II. The Population of the Region
Distribution
Sources and Nationalities
Racial Composition
Income Distribution
Recent Migrations
Long-run Trends

III. The Historical Background
Colonial Life
Colonial Industries and Agriculture
Colonial Leaders
The Revolution in New England
The Constitution and New England
Cultural Leaders of the 19th Century
The New England Economy in the 19th Century
Sectionalism and the Civil War
The Age of Big Business
The World War
New England in the 'Twenties
The Depression Years
New England and World War II — Background

IV. The Regional Economy
Agriculture — Types of Farming
Manufactures
Commerce and Finance
Forestry
Mining and Quarrying
The Fishing Industry
Trade with Other Regions

V. *Regional Problems*

Conservation — Forest, Soils, Rivers, Fish, etc.
Transportation — Air, Sea, Rail, Highways
Rural Problems — Migration, Part-time farming
Educational Problems — Youth Problems
Social Welfare — Housing, Health, Social Security
Government Problems — Town, County, State, Federal
National Defense
Economic and Social Planning — Local and Regional

VI. *Other Topics*

Most of the teachers to whom the questionnaire was sent were members of the New England Council for the Social Studies or of the New England History Teachers' Association. Care was taken to send questionnaires to several teachers in each of the large cities of New England. About half of the teachers questioned teach in the schools of Massachusetts, one fourth in the two states of Connecticut and Rhode Island, and one fourth in the three states of Maine, New Hampshire, and Vermont. This geographical distribution is roughly commensurate with the geographical distribution of the population of New England. Approximately a third of the questionnaires were sent to each major division of the public schools: the elementary grades, the junior high schools, and the senior high schools. Of the two hundred questionnaires sent out, one hundred and thirty-five were returned: forty-two by elementary-school teachers; sixty by junior high-school teachers; and thirty-three by senior high-school teachers.

The questionnaire revealed that the primary grades teach little or nothing on New England life in a regional sense because they concentrate on the home, the family, the neighborhood, the community, and children's activities.

In the fourth-grade level the teachers checked the following topics as receiving much emphasis: colonial life, colonial industries and agriculture, and colonial leaders. These topics form the nuclei for a large share of the American history taught at that level. Since a considerable portion of early American history has to do with New England, there is much emphasis upon New England colonial history in the fourth grade. This compares favorably with the textbook survey.

In the fifth-grade level, nearly every teacher checked the topics under geography and natural resources and the regional economy as receiving much emphasis. This also agrees with the geography-textbook survey for that grade level. The almost universal checking of these topics on geography and the regional economy leads the writer to believe that a unit is taught in nearly every elementary school in New England on the geography of New England, and this unit usually comes in the fifth grade and requires about three weeks' time. There are probably variations from this three weeks, but that is about the average amount of time spent on such study. The writer believes also that most of the teachers following this unit follow one of the widely used textbooks in geography and thus cover many topics briefly.

Sixth-grade teachers indicated that the major topic of study in most grade schools consisted of the historical background of New England; that is, in the study of New England life, the historical development is stressed. A few teachers — twelve — checked the topics under geography of New England as receiving much emphasis. This might mean that United States geography is studied in their sixth grades rather than in the fifth grade. Several teachers indicated that the European backgrounds of American history were studied in the sixth grade.

Seventh-grade teachers checked almost the same topics as fourth-grade teachers as receiving much emphasis, namely, colonial life, colonial industries and agriculture, and colonial leaders. This seemed to be true no matter what textbook was used. Three teachers checked the topics on geography and the regional economy. These three wrote on the back of their questionnaires that they used supplements to geography books on New England, supplements which were prepared for use in the junior high schools. Four wrote that their courses were fusion courses — probably Rugg courses — and they indicated that the textbooks did not treat New England as a region.

Eighth-grade teachers also checked topics on history dealing with colonial life. Only two checked geography and natural resources or the regional economy. Certainly little emphasis is given to a study of New England life in the eighth grade, as judged by the answers received from teachers. Four eighth-grade teachers indicated that they were using the Rugg series of fusion books and there was no treatment of New England as a region.

Since only three ninth-grade teachers returned their questionnaires, the writer hesitates to draw conclusions as to what is taught about New England on the ninth-grade level. Those high schools which teach ancient history teach little about New England, and it would seem that those which teach fusion courses place little emphasis upon New England study. One of the teachers who returned the questionnaire was from Hingham, Massachusetts, where the unusual ninth-grade program already mentioned was in progress. The other two questionnaires were from ninth-grade civics teachers who wrote that they teach something about general town government in New England, but that the major interest of their courses is community and national government.

The high-school teachers of American history, economics,

problems of democracy, sociology, and economic geography returned very few of the questionnaires; of the seventy sent out, only thirty-three were returned. Of these, thirteen wrote short notes and did not check any topics. The typical note ran something like this:

> We do not emphasize the study of New England. However, in our teaching New England is discussed incidentally with many units, and often is studied in current-events study. We teach no units on New England.

This type of note came usually from teachers of problems of democracy, economics, or American history. Of course the American history teachers usually checked the topics on colonial life under history — the same topics checked by elementary-school teachers and by junior high-school teachers. Two geography teachers answered the questionnaire and checked topics on climate, resources, and conservation problems, but each wrote that the problems were considered in a national sense and were not treated regionally. Three economics teachers checked the regional economy and wrote "only incidental references," "combined with other materials," and "treated as examples of economic problems." Four teachers of problems of democracy answered, and they indicated that no special emphasis was placed upon the study of New England regional problems. It is recognized that the returns from high-school teachers were not sufficiently widespread nor large in quantity, and therefore only limited conclusions can be drawn; but certainly no questionnaire revealed any outstanding effort to teach high-school youth the life and problems of New England.

Conclusions

From this survey of the social-studies programs of New England schools, in which outstanding leaders in the field, high-school and elementary-school state supervisors, the social-studies textbooks, and the social-studies teachers were canvassed to give the answer to the problem of what youth is taught about

New England life and problems, the following conclusions seem valid:

1. There are practically no outstanding programs of curriculum revision now in progress which are aimed at the education of New England youth for an understanding of the resources, economy, problems, or recent social trends of New England.

2. Leaders in education in New England do not know of any widespread movement to adjust the social-studies programs of New England schools to the life and problems of the youth of New England or the life of the region.

3. With the exception of isolated cases, there are no programs in existence to teach New England youth the life and problems of New England.

4. There is no evidence to show that the schools of New England use social-studies textbooks which give emphasis to the life and problems of New England. The same textbooks are used on a wide scale that are popular throughout the nation.

5. No books are used widely which present a regional interpretation of American life or a regional interpretation of New England life, although such books exist.

6. The one area of New England life which New England youth studies consistently throughout the grades is colonial life and the early settlement of New England.

7. In none of the sources of information on New England's schools and their social-studies programs did the writer find any reference to the recent developments in regional coöperation and integration.

8. The materials offered in textbooks on New England life and problems are usually sketchy, vague, and very general. Usually such materials as are presented are out of date.

The general conclusion of the survey is that New England youth learns very little or nothing, through the social-studies program of the schools, about the life and problems of New England. Through the four sources of information there should have been revealed somewhere, if it exists, a program of social education for living in New England. But it is the considered belief of the writer that no program exists which teaches New England youth the economy, resources, problems, and recent social trends of New England as a region.

CHAPTER V

WHAT NEW ENGLAND SCHOOLS OUGHT TO TEACH ABOUT NEW ENGLAND REGIONAL LIFE

THE PURPOSE of this chapter is to present a summary statement of what New England boys and girls ought to learn about the life and problems of the region through the social-studies programs of the schools. The areas on New England which are presented and summarily described here have been selected on the basis of three criteria. The first is the needs and problems and life of New England; the second criterion is the needs and problems of youth; and the third criterion is the work already done by social scientists in studying the region. Under each area will be presented an elaboration of the area, a statement of why it should be studied in New England schools, and a statement of the relevance of such study to the welfare of New England.

AREA I. THE REGIONAL RESOURCES OF NEW ENGLAND

Every New England youth should be given an opportunity to learn all he can about the basic natural resources of his region. The study of the regional resources ought to include such factors as climate, forests, rivers, lakes, minerals, the Atlantic Ocean and coastline, wild life, and the regional topography. Not only ought youth to be made aware of the existence of these resources, but he should also be conversant with the uses to which the resources have been put, and the potentialities they hold for man in this region in the future. Furthermore, he needs to appreciate the land as a basic element in the life of New England. This means that he must be familiar with the beauty of the land; and he must study the land to come to a lasting or enduring appreciation of its beauty and its usefulness. In Chapter IV evidence was presented which indicated that only in the lower grades was there much study of the resources of New England in New England schools. Surely the objective could not be attained with the study of a single unit for a few weeks in the intermediate grades. Such study is worthy of efforts and energy on the junior and senior high-school levels.

Chapter III presented a discussion which showed that several of New England's problems arise from the use to which the natural resources have been put in the past and should be put in the future. The forests, the lakes, the rivers, the beaches, and other resources need careful husbanding to retain the wild life, to sustain the recreational industry, and to provide other basic materials for local industries. Moreover, there is some evidence to indicate the deterioration of resources in nature which add to the beauty of New England. The region's youth needs to be made aware of these problems so that it may make some attack upon them when it comes to adulthood. For the welfare of the region itself there is need to educate youth to the resources, the problems of their conservation, their potentialities for the future, and their basic role in human existence.

The youth of New England needs to understand the regional resources in order to come to self-realization itself. That is, youth needs to have beauty, and one source of such beauty can come through appreciation and understanding of nature. Moreover, for purposes of economic and vocational preparation, young people need to understand the foundations of their vocations, and to a large extent the resources of nature underly the work of all New Englanders. As a member of society a youth will have to help make decisions concerning the use of natural resources. Such decisions will be more valuable if a youth has a good working knowledge of the resources.

The regionalists are almost universal in their emphasis upon study of nature's resources in each particular region. It would be almost impossible to make a regional survey without including a survey of the setting and resources of the region. Nearly all problems arising out of land utilization, industry, and agriculture must be related to the resources of a region. Thus, a considered study of New England regional life and problems would be incomplete without a study of the endowment of nature and its value and role in the life of the people.

AREA II. THE REGIONAL POPULATION

The second major area which social-studies programs should emphasize for New England youth is that which deals with the people of New England. Chapter IV indicated that little or no emphasis is placed upon the study of the regional population or New England's human resources. The topics which should be included in such study are the distribution of the population, the occupational distribution of the people, the incomes of the people, the trends in population growth, the nationalities and sources of population, and the movements of people within and into and out of the region.

Obviously, the purpose behind all regional planning and the test of regional well-being should be revealed in the general welfare of the people who inhabit a region. The regional scientists are intensely interested in the kind of people that live in a region, where they came from, what their folkways are, what their living levels are, and what their chief ways of making a living are. Much of the study of population is statistical in nature, but it is of great importance, for, in the last analysis, the people of a region constitute an enormous resource in themselves, and they constitute the chief reason for planning for the future. No regional study would be complete without a study of the population.

A well-informed and competent citizen needs to know the characteristics of the people with whom he is to associate. He must learn to work with a variety of people in New England — people of varying religious faiths, nationalities, and cultural backgrounds. He will be a better citizen in New England and will be much better able to help solve some of the pressing intercultural problems of the region if he has an understanding of the total regional population. Moreover, a competent citizen needs to understand the problems of rural–urban nature, such as part-time farming, transportation, and the making of prices for farm goods, the provision of markets in the cities, and the total picture of rural–urban interdependence. The study of the population of New England by New England youth ought to help produce a realistic tolerance and a basis for intercultural coöperation for the welfare of the whole region. Such study should aid in the development of a social sensitivity that is vital for the consideration of the region's problems.

For the well-being of New England, its citizenry are going to need specific information about population trends which will help them participate in formulating public policies concerning welfare programs, housing and health programs, educational programs, and conservation programs. Urban and rural planning of the sort needed in New England and most likely to come with the development of transportation in the post-war era will be dangerously unrealistic if the citizenry of the region are uninformed as to the character of its people.

Area III. The History of New England

Evidence has been presented which shows that the youth of New England spends considerable time in the study of the colonial settlement and early development of New England as a region. It has been pointed out, however, that little or no attention is being given to the study of the development of the economy, politics, social life, and character of the nineteenth and twentieth centuries in New England. Youth is made aware of the hardihood, character, and philosophy of the Puritans, but lacks real and specific information on the Irish migrations, the Polish migrations, the Italian migrations, or the infusion of French-Canadians, Nova-Scotians, and Jews. Young people understand the development of early mills on the waterways of New England, but they lack specific information about the development of agriculture and industry and commerce in the late nineteenth and early twentieth centuries. Scarcely mentioned are such developments as the rise of big cities, the decline of agriculture, and the development of modern transportation. Such facets of New England's history should be understood by all New England youths.

In all regional studies, historical references are abundant. Often the best clue to the future is contained in the history of a region. At least historical study gives perspective. The experience of a people in using and living in a region usually proves valuable to present inhabitants, and therefore, for the regionalist, such understanding is basic to understanding the present scene.

Youth needs social perspective. It needs to be familiar with the eras of the past in its region. It needs to have a feeling that its region has accomplished much, that it has met and solved its problems before. Young people need the balance which such study can bring in their own lives. New England has had three centuries of history. There is much in it that can give youth hope and courage. It can give youth in the region a basis for patriotism, a basis for loving and appreciating the region, and it can produce a basis for security and a challenge for the future. But the study of New England's history ought not be the recounting of the kinds of facts and ideas that produce a regional exclusiveness or a selfish sectionalism. A study of New England's history ought to reveal the futility of that type of thinking, and it ought to abolish some of the provincialism which now exists.

The regional history that schools need to teach youth in New England should bring New England youth to see their region as an organic part of the total American scene. It has been a region which has enriched America in the past, and it holds possibilities for a continuous enrichment of the national life. Yet, this connection with the national scene should reveal the character and color of New England as a part of the national scene. The New England region needs inner bolstering to banish the shibboleths of regional decadence or of pessimism about the future which have been spread abroad in the periodical literature of the nation within the past two decades. For this reason, the whole population of the future which is now in the schools needs, for the welfare of New England, some study of the past which will produce a realistic optimism in the future of New England. This does not mean a giddy optimism. It means that New Englanders have a region which has lived through crises before, and it has the resources, both human and natural, to meet crisis today and in the future.

AREA IV. THE REGIONAL ECONOMY OF NEW ENGLAND

Social-studies programs need to present to the youth of New England a realistic account of the ways of making a living in New England. No youth should be allowed to plan for work that may be discontinued because of technological changes or regional maladjustment. Moreover, schools have a responsibility to society and to each youth to inform young people of the trends which seem likely to determine the occupations of the future. At present New England schools are not giving New England youth adequate instruction in the characteristics of New England's economy.

To understand the social life and problems of a society it is imperative that one consider the economic foundations of that society. The ways of making a living, of trading, of transporting, of producing, of distributing, and of consuming are the significant facets of a region's economy. No regional survey would be complete without such information.

Youth needs economic education relative to the home region. It needs to be aware of economic changes, problems, and conditions in the region in order to make some realistic preparation for such phenomena. This knowledge is basic to the welfare of every working individual.

Planning and conceiving a future for New England as a region requires that every citizen have a basic understanding of what the economy of the region is, what it can be in terms of the people, their resources, and their character, and the relation of the New England economy to the nation and world. As has been suggested in Chapter III, the next few years in New England will require changes in occupations and industries if the region is to remain stable and productive. Planning for new industries adapted to the regional resources, the development of transportation systems, and the related problems should be and must be the concern of every citizen.

AREA V. THE GOVERNMENTS OF NEW ENGLAND

The complexities of government in New England were stressed in Chapter III, and attention was called to the fact that here are large metropolitan governments, small town governments, large and small state governments, and the various facets of federal government, all working for the general welfare of the population. There is duplication of effort, some waste, and much need for coöperation. Social and economic planning has become an important task of all governments in the past decade, and it seems likely that government planning will continue to be an important factor in the life of New England. The social-studies programs of New England schools need to emphasize the kinds and types of governments in New England, the ways in which these governments are related, and the problems which confront them in working for the welfare of the region. Much more study is needed dealing with government planning on the local, state, regional, and national levels.

It is difficult to understand the total social complex which is now New England apart from a study of the governments and means of social control present in the region. The public policies which are manifested by governments in New England grow out of the social life and needs of the people, and it is well-nigh impossible to comprehend government or social life in a region without close study of each and their relations.

Youth needs understanding of the role of governments in solving social problems, and needs to understand what relations future citizens will have in creating public policy. It will be a rare citizen in the future who will not have many contacts with the federal government agencies which make New England a region. It would seem that youth needs to study the governments of New England for their own self-realization as the governments assume more and more importance in the lives of ordinary citizens.

New England needs to improve its governments, and the relations between all types of government need to be made more workable and efficient. The role of the federal government in social welfare, in education, in conservation, in transportation, and in many other areas demands that more than the study of the structure of governments be studied in New England's schools. New England needs a citizenry that can understand the problems of government, that can shape good governmental policies, and that can make decisions as to when government should handle a social problem. Many of New England's problems are of the type that demand government planning, but many can be solved through proper private enterprise and planning. A knowledge of government will help citizens make important decisions on such matters.

Area VI. The Regional Culture of New England

Social-studies programs should do their part in New England to introduce New England youth to the finest in cultural expression in the region. Music, the arts, literature, the little theaters, and museums are all examples of the kind of cultural factors which the social-studies programs could reasonably help interpret for youth. To accomplish this objective the social studies will probably have to utilize more than the typical objective, empirical teaching materials, and introduce intuitive, impressionistic types of learning situations. Young people need to learn the background of the beauty that is present in New England. They need to feel that they belong to something that is organically and psychologically real, something that is worth living for, believing in, and planning for. They need the feeling of attachment to a culture, a landscape, an environment, or, as the Germans have it, a *heimat*.

There is a grandeur about the great centers of learning in New England, the Boston Symphony Orchestra, the colonial architecture, and the white churches set near town halls and village greens. It rises somewhat above the local antiquarian societies and becomes and is a part of the whole heritage of western culture. New England is more than the Puritan Tradition, the historic shrines, or the home of certain minor poets. It is a region which is now carrying part of the heritage of western culture in its libraries, museums, colleges, universities, research centers, theaters, and publishing houses. Besides, there is a natural charm about the region which young people need to feel. The delight which travelers get from the tang of the seacoast towns, the October foliage, and the minute and disorganized farmsteads ought to be a part of the personality and emotions of New England youth.

This attachment to the region may be challenged by some for fear that it will inculcate an intolerance toward other regions or a provincialism on a regional basis. However, those who are able to understand and appreciate their own culture are usually those who have the depth to appreciate the life and character of other regions. Moreover, other study would give evidence that New England is but part of a total national scene, and that it owes its richness and character to being a part of western culture.

A regional people need have no compunctions about seeing to it that the youth of the region develop a love and an appreciation of the region. Such an attachment is basic for the welfare of the region and for the welfare of youth. New England youth needs to come to a richer and more appreciative feeling toward New England. This feeling is needed to replace cynicism, and to build a foundation of inner strength for the individual.

AREA VII. THE REGIONAL PROBLEMS OF NEW ENGLAND

The assumption that it is the responsibility of the social studies to acquaint youth with the important problems of society is widely accepted today. This does not mean that youth ought to study problems that are beyond its grasp or that immature minds should attempt to grapple with every social problem. The typical high-school youth, however, needs a knowledge of the pressing problems and issues of his community, state, and region. As an adult he will not usually have the time or the facilities for gaining objective evidence from which to make decisions on important problems. Thus the school has the special responsibility in a democracy of acquainting youth with problems that are of long-range and fundamental importance to society. Knowing that great human problems exist in society ought not discourage youth from appreciating the values of their society, but rather, should help to sensitize youth to their responsibility in seeking solutions for social problems.

The pressing problems of New England are not given the emphasis in the schools of New England which they ought to receive. Such problems as government planning, social welfare, medical care, regional adjustment, conservation of resources, and general regional well-being are not given adequate treatment in the social-studies programs of New England schools.

One of the principal ways in which humanity makes progress is through the continuous solution of its problems. The widespread study, description, and analysis of social problems are hallmarks of mature nations. Scholarship demands freedom for objective research on social problems, and a democratic nation guarantees to each individual the right to participate in the discussion of issues. Is it not then the duty of the common schools to give youth practice in the study and discussion of problems in terms of the maturity of youth and the evidence available on problems? It is in schools that youth can be objective, that there are materials for study, time for discussion, and the atmosphere of humane consideration. New England's major problems which need solution ought to be presented to youth in New England if later as adults they are to grapple with these problems. The welfare of youth, the welfare of the region, and indeed the welfare of the nation, are dependent upon an enlightened and sensitive citizenry that can solve common problems.

Summary

Here has been presented a summary of what it is thought New England youth ought to learn about New England as a region. The topics or areas are the resources, the people, the economy, the polity, the history, the culture, the problems. The bases for selection of these areas of study on New England were the problems of New England as a region, the needs of youth, and the works and procedures of the social scientists. It was indicated that little or no emphasis was given to the study of these areas in New England schools. The outline of content contained in this chapter will, it is believed, aid youth in New England to come to a better understanding of the region which nurtures them, and further, such study will make a contribution to the welfare of New England and the nation in the long run.

CHAPTER VI

PLANS AND MATERIALS FOR ADJUSTING THE SOCIAL-STUDIES PROGRAMS OF NEW ENGLAND SCHOOLS TO THE LIFE AND PROBLEMS OF NEW ENGLAND

THE DISCUSSION in this chapter will concern itself with the following problems: (1) Where can the seven areas of content on New England, presented in Chapter V, be introduced in the social-studies programs of New England schools? (2) What teaching materials are available for teaching the regional life of New England? (3) What teaching materials are needed for teaching the regional life of New England? (4) What are the implications of this study for teacher training, for regional coöperation in educational planning, and for national educational policy in American schools?

INTRODUCING THE SEVEN AREAS OF CONTENT ON
NEW ENGLAND

Elementary Schools. It has already been established that the study of New England life in the elementary grades deals largely with the geography and the early history of the region. However, in these two areas the study of New England is general, broad, and lacking in specificity. In some books, it will be recalled, a dozen cities are discussed in one page. Such study for a child is apt to degenerate into mere verbalism and memory exercises. In the historical study there is little or no specific reference to actual people and what they did in colonial times. It is recommended, therefore, that in the fourth, fifth, and sixth grades the study of New England be made much more concrete for children. To enliven and enrich the study, it is recommended that:

1. The lives of selected colonial leaders be studied.
2. The types of economic activities be studied.
3. The types of social life in rural and urban centers be studied.
4. The physical features of New England, such as rivers, mountains, coastline, harbors, and other specific geographic phenomena receive more study.
5. The relations between the local community and the whole region be indicated through field trips, films, and reading activities.
6. The historical shrines and cultural institutions which are near each school be visited.
7. The elementary school begin the study of the variety of peoples who live in the community, state, and region.

Some of the foregoing recommendations can be followed out by adding new units. Others can be met by adding new activities in units now being taught in the elementary schools. The principal objective is to use the capacities of elementary-school children in the wisest way to lay foundations for future study, and to enlarge the child's conception of the society and environment which surround him.

The study of society on the elementary-school level ought to be made as specific as possible. Many of the generalizations and relationships stressed in elementary-school geography books are beyond the capacities of the age level. Specifically, however, children can learn about various land forms and geographic features. Children can understand early colonial life more vividly and more appreciatively through stories of people who lived in colonial times. By making models of colonial houses and colonial towns, and by visiting historical monuments built in colonial times, children can come to a more realistic understanding of the colonial period. In the elementary grades the beginnings of such skills as map reading and interpretation, library work, the making of graphs and charts, and the beginnings of committee reports after reading are laid. To study New England life and environment in the elementary schools all of the kinds of activities which produce realistic understandings should be utilized. Maps of the community and of the region and state can be introduced in the fifth or sixth grade, and many schools have introduced them successfully in the fourth grade. Films can be used to bring ideas to children very effectively. The study of racial and national groups can be started in the elementary grades because children have not yet acquired some of the intolerances which adults have. There are many materials on New England available for the elementary school, but others are needed. Both will be discussed in a later section of this chapter.

Here is a list of some unit titles which should help to indicate the kinds of learning about New England that elementary-school children can profitably pursue. Many schools now have similar units. These units could be added in a fusion program or they could be added in a subject-matter program. Some of them were suggested in a previous publication.[1]

1. New England's Water Resources.
2. A Year of Life on a New England Farm.
3. Transportation and Communication in New England.
4. Life in a Colonial Family in New England.
5. The People of Mytown and New England.
6. New England's Mountains and Forests.
7. New England's Wildlife.
8. Famous New Englanders of Colonial Times.
9. Life in a Colonial Town in New England.
10. The White Man and the Indians in Colonial New England.

Junior High Schools. The most important subjects in the social studies in the junior high schools are American history

[1] Royce H. Knapp, "American Regionalism and Social Education," *Social Education*, December 1942, p. 365.

and geography. Accordingly, recommendations will be made which can be adapted to these major areas of study. Since in the junior high years pupils have a foundation of skills to work with, and since their reading abilities have increased, more difficult subjects can be dealt with. The relationships in geography and time concepts of history are more easily handled at this level than in the elementary schools. There is still, however, need for practice of skills, particularly in the use of books, in the use of maps, in recitation, in coöperative enterprises, and in the making of oral reports. The beginnings of vocational guidance should be laid in the junior high-school years. Pupils have usually traveled further, have had more experiences, and have a wider range of interests in the life around them.

It was indicated in Chapter IV that little or no attention is given in the schools to the study of nineteenth- and twentieth-century developments in New England, and that little attention is given to the study of economic activities in New England. To remedy this situation, it is recommended that in the junior high schools:

1. Attention be given to the kinds of economic activities in which New Englanders engage.
2. Emphasis be placed upon the development of New England during the nineteenth and twentieth centuries.
3. Some problems of conservation and of New England as a region be introduced for study.
4. The relation of New England to the nation and to the world be studied more intensively.
5. Schools give opportunity for pupils to study some of the problems of acculturation present in New England.
6. Schools begin the study of town governments, of state governments, and of the relationships between these and the national government.
7. Emphasis be placed upon the great cultural institutions of New England and their development during the nineteenth and twentieth centuries.

Of the seven major areas of content, it would seem that history, economy, governments, culture, and (more cautiously) problems, would find their way into the junior high schools. While the elementary schools gave their attention to certain facets of early history, simple geography, culture, and people, the junior high school could carry on with more difficult topics in some of these areas. The general objective is to allocate the areas of content according to the increasing maturity of the pupils in the schools, so that specific and concrete ideas are taught in the lower grades, and more difficult relational ideas are taught in the upper grades. The following unit titles are typical of the kinds which can be used in the junior high-school years:

1. Specialized Farming in New England.
2. Immigration During the Nineteenth Century in New England.
3. The Role of the Sea in New England Life.
4. The Metal Goods Industries of New England.
5. New England Town Government.
6. Regional Organizations in New England.
7. The Metropolitan Centers of New England.
8. Recreational Activities in New England.
9. Raw Materials for New England Industries.
10. Colleges and Universities in New England.

Senior High Schools. The introduction of the seven areas of content into the curriculum of the high school will depend largely upon the courses offered and the school itself. But certain factors should be taken into account in making recommendations for the high-school level. High-school students are nearer their vocational choice. Many of them will not go on to college. Most of them are reading as well as they will ever read. Their experiences are more varied, and many are already working. The locality of the school will make some difference, too, but there are certain ideas which all young people should have, no matter where they live in New England. The recommendations here will be based upon subjects offered in the ordinary schools of New England.

American history is taught in every school in New England, and it offers several opportunities for including topics on the life and problems of the region. The following recommendations are made for American history study in New England schools:

1. Schools should emphasize the recent history of New England in the rise of big business, the First World War, the inflation years of the twenties, and the depression years of the thirties.
2. Schools should emphasize in the American history course the evolution of commerce and industry in New England to show how it has changed during the past three centuries.
3. The American history course should deal with the rise of regionalism and of regional coöperation, with special references to New England.
4. The contributions of New England to the political, social, and economic life of the nation during the past should be part of the American history course.

Obviously, there are limitations on the amount of information on New England which can be added or taught in the American history course. But there are many opportunities for planned incidental study of New England in the study of larger topics treating the whole nation. Moreover, the inclusion of topics or of units on the history of New England ought to help young New Englanders understand the nation better because they will understand their own part of the nation better. It is recommended that at least one unit of the American history course in New England high schools deal with New England, preferably a unit in recent history.

Geography is not universally required as a high-school subject in New England. It is usually taught as an elective or as a required subject for commercial students. Recently, the National Council for the Social Studies issued a bulletin on a wartime policy for the social studies. One of the recommendations was that one year of social geography be required of all secondary-school pupils. This requirement should, it is believed, be made effective in New England schools. Certainly the course in geography on the high-school level offers many opportunities for educating the pupil realistically about his society and his region. In the courses in commercial or economic geography now being taught, there are several opportunities for teaching facets of New England regional life. The following recommendations are made in terms of the courses as now taught:

1. Courses in high-school geography should emphasize the conservation problems of New England and their relation to regional welfare.
2. Courses in high-school geography should place emphasis upon the study of the bases for the manufacturing industries of New England.
3. The interregional trade and commerce of New England and its geographical foundation should be studied in high-school geography courses.
4. Courses in geography should emphasize the study of New England's resources, their uses today, and their potentialities for the future.

In order to leave more time in the high-school course in geography for the consideration of vital regional problems, it is recommended that the study of the principles of geography and elementary mathematical geography be emphasized in the elementary and junior-high grades. Furthermore, pupils would gain if in all social studies use were made of their map skills learned in geography. The high-school course in geography should be realistic in dealing with the problems of the environment surrounding youth and with problems which will affect young people after they leave school. Units on conservation, manufactures and raw materials, transportation and commerce,

PLANS AND MATERIALS 111

and the resources of New England should be part of the high-school geography course.

The course in problems of democracy is widely taught in New England, as it is throughout the nation. This course as taught deals primarily with a series of national problems, social, economic, and political. There must be some limit to what can be taught in one year to a junior or senior class in high school in a problems-of-democracy course, but the course certainly ought to give some background for the study of the region in which the young people will live. Also, many of the national-problems studies have local applications and local characteristics. These should be emphasized. It is believed that the boys and girls of New England have the right and the maturity by the time they reach senior high school to discuss intelligently and to study effectively for personal and for social reasons some of the following problems which now exist in New England. It is recommended that these problems be considered:

1. How can the people of New England develop their governments so that an effective common attack can be made on the region's problems?
2. How can adequate medical care, adequate housing, adequate nutrition, and adequate education be provided for the people of New England?
3. How can the diverse races and nationalities of New England coöperate more effectively?
4. What relation should exist between urban and rural areas? What are their responsibilities toward each other?
5. What is the role of the New England region in the life of the nation?

These are not easy problems. There are no ready-made answers for them. Yet they are the types of problems which high-school pupils will have to consider, if they exercise their citizenship, within a few years after graduation from high school. The pressing and persistent problems of New England deserve all the study that young citizens can make of them while in high school.

Economics courses offer opportunities to a few high-school students. Such courses are usually elective, unless they are required in the commercial course. For those who take economics in New England schools, the study of a considerable amount of information about the regional economy of New England ought to be required. This study should be much more advanced than the study of the regional economy in the junior high school. It ought to emphasize the totality of the regional economy, and the interdependence of parts of the economy. It ought to emphasize facets of the economy which are pertinent to the lives of the students. The following recommendations are made for including new emphases in the course in economics in the high schools of New England:

1. A study of the many ways in which a living can be made in New England.
2. A study of the conditions and trends of New England industries.
3. A study of the relation of regional planning to the total economy.
4. A study of the emerging problems in the economy of New England.

Sociology is not widely taught in New England high schools, but for those schools which do teach the subject and for those who may wish to teach it, the following recommendations are made:

1. There should be study of the various cultural groups of New England, with emphasis upon their contributions to New England life, their problems, and their characteristics.
2. Sociology courses could well emphasize many of the social problems in the problems-of-democracy course.
3. Sociology courses could emphasize problems of living in rural areas.

PLANS AND MATERIALS

The extent to which additional topics or units can be taught on the life and problems of New England will be dependent largely upon the local situation. It will require planning on the part of all teachers in a high school to mesh the program so that there will not be overlapping, but there should be interrelations. One way to attack the problem would be for the teachers in a high school to work together on a series of units dealing with the seven major areas of content on New England. Then, after producing several resource units, some division could be made so that most of the material would be taught in the high school. It might be that some courses would teach an idea only incidentally, but another course would teach a major unit on the idea. The making of a curriculum of social studies requires the work of all the teachers. In the present monograph only areas for emphasis and suggestions for places of emphasis can be made. Following is a list of unit titles of the type which could be used in high school courses:

1. The Interdependence of City and Farm in New England.
2. The Cultural Diversities of the People of New England.
3. Regional Planning in New England.
4. Problems of Selected New England Industries.
5. Agricultural Problems in New England.
6. Problems of Big Cities in New England.
7. New England in the Depression Years.
8. New England and World War II.
9. The Rise of Giant Industries in New England.
10. The Political History of New England.
11. Opportunities for Youth in New England.
12. Housing Problems in New England.
13. Rural Planning in New England.
14. Problems of Transportation and Communication in New England.
15. New England in the Post-War Era.
16. Cultural Centers of New England.

17. Labor Problems and Conditions in New England.
18. New England and the Federal Government.

It would be almost impossible to have every high-school pupil in New England study with the same intensiveness all seven areas of content, but every school should examine its program of social studies to see what is being taught about New England, and what ought to be and can be added. There are many correlations which can and ought to be made between the social studies program and other studies. Art courses could give opportunities for expression of artistic and aesthetic ideas about New England. English courses offer opportunities for reading poetry, drama, and novels which deal with New England. Courses in agriculture offer opportunities for study of the agricultural problems of New England. Wherever such correlations can be made in a high school, it would seem that the study of New England life would be much enriched.

Some new courses might be developed on the high-school level as electives in social studies. Such a plan is being worked out in Brookline, Massachusetts, where one half-year study of the life and problems of New England is to be offered in the coming years. This course will consist of probably a half-dozen units on the region — units named after topics similar to the seven content areas — and will serve as an introduction to a more intensive study. The ninth grade civics course at Hingham, Massachusetts, is almost the same in that it concentrates on Hingham in the first semester, and on New England in the second half year. These courses on New England are valuable in that they give students knowledge which is basic to good citizenship.

In the foregoing recommendations the seven major areas of content on New England — resources, people, economy, polity, history, culture, problems — have been recognized as important necessary additions to the social-studies programs of New Englang schools. General recommendations have been made for each area of the program, and specific unit titles and content have been suggested as types which illustrate the general recommendations.

The Problem of Materials

The social-studies program is necessarily dependent upon adequate and reliable sources and teaching materials, and this study would not be complete without stressing the materials available to implement such recommendations as have been made, and the materials needed for implementation. As will be seen there are in existence many kinds and a considerable amount of teaching material for most levels.

Available Resources. A classified list of available teaching materials on New England is included in the Appendices. The number of books in the non-fiction field which can be used by school pupils is limited. There are nine books dealing with the history, geography, government, and state history of various parts of New England for the junior-high-school grades and two geography supplements of about one hundred pages each. One text on citizenship contains a ninety-four page supplement on New England. For the senior high school, there are no books that deal with New England in a complete manner. There are books about famous towns, famous people, and some historical works. There seems to be no accurate non-fiction on New England for elementary schools.

There is a good bibliography of fiction, however. Thirteen books of stories are available for elementary schools. Eight books are available for junior high schools; and there are many novels and biographical studies of a historical nature available for high-school use. It should be noted that many of the books, pamphlets, and periodicals that are addressed to adults are of value also to high-school pupils. Thus many of the books appearing in the major bibliography of this study could be used in high schools.

Five films on New England are listed in Appendix E. Two

of these deal with colonial life and three deal with the fishing industry. There are commercial advertising films available from some of the industrial firms of New England, but not all of these are adaptable to the classroom.

The maps for studying New England are rather limited in number, but those that have been made for schools are excellent. They are physical-political and include the whole region. Some maps of states are available from some map companies, and the various states publish highway maps that are very good. The New England Regional Planning Commission has assembled a sizable set of good maps on New England.

All of these materials are listed in the Appendices, and in some cases they are described. For materials for high schools the publications listed in the major bibliography under the New England Regional Planning Commission should be valuable.

Materials Needed. Several kinds of teaching aids and resources are needed if teachers are to teach the regional life of New England satisfactorily. The following are recommended.

1. *A Handbook on New England.* A handbook which presents summaries of statistical data, recognized sources, historic data, and information on industry, agriculture, government, and other facets of New England life, in encyclopedic form or as an almanac, is needed for references by teacher and pupils. A handbook of this type should be regularly revised by competent authorities after each United States Census. It might well be valuable to others than schools, a fact which might justify a private publisher in bringing it out.

2. *A Variety of New Maps on New England.* The maps which are now available are limited largely to political and physical types. There are no large maps now available to schools which show agricultural production, rainfall distribution, temperatures, natural vegetation, conservation problems, or transportation problems. In some of the leading scholarly books on New England, maps of this type appear on a small scale. A series of such maps for wall displays ought to be de-

veloped for school use. Maps have always constituted a major tool for the social studies, and there is sufficient evidence and material to create a series of valuable teaching maps on New England.

3. *Films, Slides, and Pictorial Materials.* With the development of very excellent films in recent years, it would seem that more of them might deal with the life and problems of New England. Films could be made to cover each of the several areas of content on New England life, and these could be made available to many schools through rotation and rental. In addition, good slides are needed for projection. Sometimes schools can make their own slides or have them made from photographs at little expense. Another area of pictorial materials which offers much for schools is aerial-photography. This type of picture presents several square miles of countryside, or it can present a whole city from the air so that the configuration and arrangement of streets and sections can be studied. The experience which the war photographers have gained in the Army and Navy should help in the development of these materials for schools. The production of moving pictures, and other pictorial materials, ought, however, to be guided by competent educational leaders, skilled technicians, and experts on New England. Coöperation between these groups should produce excellent materials.

4. *Resource Units on New England Life and Problems.* The resource unit idea could well be applied to the problem of materials on New England. A resource unit is a reservoir of information, ideas, materials, and procedures upon which a teacher can draw in securing assistance in planning for the teaching of particular units in the classroom. Usually there is included a discussion of the unit for the teacher, a series of suggestions for organizing the teaching procedures, a list of learning situations, a list of good teaching materials, and suggestions for evaluation. Such units are of considerable value to teachers for they afford an opportunity to adjust the teaching

materials to the local situation. If a series of such units could be developed around the major areas suggested in Chapter IV they could be of value to teachers everywhere in the region. Such units help produce flexibility, and they are usually adaptable to several subjects within a given grade level.

5. *Pupil Materials on New England Occupations.* The tendency to begin the program of vocational guidance and education in the junior high-school years posits another need for a certain type of pupil materials on that level. A series of bulletins or pamphlets ought to be developed for junior high-school pupils on the various occupations of New England. There are several books and many pamphlets for pupils of this age which deal with occupations in terms of the nation, but most of them deal with general types of work. For example, New England boys and girls need pamphlet material or bulletins on part-time farming, on work in recreational industries, or on sea occupations. Such materials would help give occupations place and environment.

6. *Elementary-School Books.* For the intermediate grades there is need to develop some good non-fiction books on New England. Such books ought to be developed around specific activities of people in New England or around the natural setting. Books should be produced for elementary schools which deal with the forests, the Atlantic Ocean, the rivers, the wild life, the mountains, and other natural features of the New England region. They should be well illustrated with maps and pictures.

Another type of book which should be written for New England elementary schools is the story book dealing with a historical period or era. Although the stories are on the level of elementary school children, their settings can be accurate. The historical novel is exciting for adults. The historical story could be made exciting and interesting for children. Stories of children in colonial times, of the sea, of any historical period, should prove valuable in that they would enliven the interests of children and help to give them a more colorful, vivid interpretation of New England life and culture. These materials should be developed by educators, writers, specialists, and teachers working together. They should be in harmony with the interests and capacities of children and the major ideas which the schools are attempting to teach.

7. *Senior High-School Textbook on New England.* For those schools that wish to add an elective half course on New England there is no textbook at present. For those schools which wish to add units throughout the social-studies program in the high schools, a textbook on the seven areas of New England life could be used in more than one course. That is, the history unit could be taught in history courses, the resources unit in geography, the economics unit in economics courses, and so on. It would be one way for schools to know that young people will come in contact with a wide range of materials on New England. Such a book ought to be written in terms of the interests and needs of the high-school student. It could serve as a reference for many courses, and as the textbook for a course on New England. It would aid teachers in many courses because the materials would be presented in the usual style for students and for teaching purposes. It would save considerable time for individual teachers in the high schools also.

8. *Special Pictorial Materials for the Primary Grades.* Since what can be taught about New England in the primary grades is limited by the children's reading ability and immaturity, there is not the need for reading materials that there is on other levels. Picture books which show various kinds of life in New England could be developed, however, and picture books on New England wild life, the ocean, the natural landscape, and other factors in nature could well be utilized in primary grades. This type of teaching material could be developed in harmony with the customary community and neighborhood studies which are carried on in most primary grades. Comparisons between the local community and other communities could be made on

a simple level, with pictures of birds, trees, houses, streets, and so on. Films and slides for primary grades could be developed also.

Recommendations for Teacher Training

Undoubtedly the social-studies teacher is the most vital link in planning for social education. It is the teacher who presents materials to pupils, who motivates pupils, who assigns tasks to pupils, who creates the learning situations, and who creates the actual curriculum of the school. Consequently, this study would be incomplete without making recommendations for the training of teachers in New England to teach youth the significant factors in the life and problems of New England.

Teachers need continuous stimulation and new information if they are to be vital in the social-studies program. They must themselves know the competent authorities on New England who are familiar with New England's problems, and they must themselves have reflected upon these problems and the trends which seem likely to determine New England's future. The extension courses of colleges and universities for in-service training of teachers ought to make available to teachers the scholars and authorities on New England life through courses and lectures. Perhaps a traveling seminar could be set up to visit various localities at varying times on a schedule. Another way in which teachers can keep themselves informed is through individual reading and study. The best books and materials available are listed in the Appendices below. Teachers could make use of larger libraries and could borrow books for a longer time if they would make special arrangements. Moreover, the professional library of every New England teacher of the social studies ought to contain one or two books on New England such as *New England's Prospect*, or one of James Truslow Adams' histories. These suggestions are for teachers in training.

For teachers who are preparing to teach the social studies in New England schools there should be arranged in the teacher-training institutions some kind of schedule and a group of courses which would acquaint New England teachers with the life and problems of New England. Courses in geography, history, economics, sociology, and government ought to treat regionalism in American life. By careful guidance and recommendation, schools of education could encourage New England teachers to take such courses. Also, teachers in education courses should become familiar with the increasing number of educational studies of regionalism and regional planning.

RECOMMENDATIONS FOR REGIONAL COÖPERATION

It was indicated in Chapter III that there has been a tendency for various agencies to coöperate on a regional basis in New England. There is no reason why schools ought not to coöperate to solve their common problems. Already many organizations exist which could serve as the media for coöperation. The various professional organizations bring teachers and administrators together for discussion and study. So far, however, there has not developed any large coöperative undertaking aimed at adjusting the social-studies programs of New England schools to the life and problems of the region. The New England Council for the Social Studies has undertaken in a small way to serve as a regional organization for the exchange of information and ideas among teachers. Its publication, the *New England Councilor*, serves as a medium for exchange, but not to any great extent. The New England Council for the Social Studies, the New England History Teachers Association, and the New England Geographical Conference could, by working together, evaluate units and teaching aids on New England and plan their distribution. Such coöperation would recognize the value of individual contributions of all schools, for when a school produced a valuable piece of work it could be exchanged and made available to other schools. The three groups of social-studies teachers have already produced a coöperative meeting, and there is hope that further coöperation will be forthcoming in the future.

Not only do social-studies teachers need to work together, but they need to work with other agencies for the common welfare of their communities and region. They should be familiar with the aims and objectives and work of all agencies working for the well-being of New England, and add weight through their opinions to the work and objectives of other agencies. Social-studies teachers, particularly, should be aware of other types of work carried on for the betterment of regional life. Such awareness should improve teaching, and it should bring teachers into the mesh of human activities and into a finer realization of their own citizenship.

American Regionalism and National Welfare

By accepting the philosophy of regionalism, educators do not accept a philosophy of sectional self-interest. There is inherent in regionalism an idea of nationalism, but it is not a narrow nationalism. It means accepting the idea that America is vast, rich, and varied; that it is a nation in which environments are different; that ways of living and working are different; but that it is precisely this diversity that creates the richness, both human and natural, that is America. It means accepting the idea of interdependence and the values which arise from interdependence. For, when people know they are dependent upon other people, when they see the value of coöperation among regions, the idea becomes important. The idea of interdependence is needed today as never before, in a world in which guns have been blazing for freedom, democracy, and the rights of mankind to be interdependent and to coöperate. Recognition of cultural diversity — in the nation and in the world — and the creation of the feeling everywhere that this is one of the great good things humanity has, ought to enrich human life and not stifle it. The earth is rich because of its diversities. Regionalism in a world sense, or in a national sense, means a recognition that life is rich and valuable, and that humanity is ennobled because of variety in human culture, natural environments, and human values.

The national welfare is best fostered when the people of the nation see the nation in the most realistic manner. Acting with the best information possible, the people in a democracy make the policies, live the values, and regenerate themselves through education. In this sense, then, regionalism holds a significant hope to educators and to the national welfare. It means that education can take place in terms of the youth and the people of a region. It means that people can set themselves at the task of creating a regional culture in America, a culture that does not suffer from mechanism, metropolitanism, sectionalism, or any other similar *ism*. It means that schools will attune themselves to the life which surrounds them, and at the same time contribute to nation and world. Basically, the idea can be illustrated in some such simple manner as this: the Chinese boy living on the broad plain of the Hwang Ho will do his part for civilization, for China, and for himself by understanding his environment, his regional culture, and by making a continuous effort to improve it and regenerate it. The New England boy ought, in the same manner, plan for a life in his region attuned to his regional environment. On such lives, and on such aspirations, perhaps the destiny of mankind rests, and out of such living ought to come "the century of the common man."

Schools have a vital role to play in the coming century. It is their enduring task to present truthfully, critically, clearly, and proudly, the life and culture of society to youth. By accomplishing this task, the schools will have contributed tremendously to the conservation and continuous regeneration of their communities, regions, and world.

APPENDICES

APPENDIX A

Letter of Inquiry Sent to New England State Supervisors and Social-Studies Leaders

HARVARD UNIVERSITY
GRADUATE SCHOOL OF EDUCATION

Lawrence Hall, Kirkland Street
Cambridge, Massachusetts

The writer is undertaking a study of materials and plans for adjusting the social studies programs in New England schools to the life and problems of the region. An important part of the study deals with recent curricular trends which might reflect this movement in the social studies.

To ascertain what is now being done, the following questions are being sent to you and about thirty other leaders in education in New England.

1. Do you know of any curriculum revision programs now in progress in the elementary or secondary schools of (the state) which are aimed at acquainting youth with the resources, economy, problems, and recent social trends of New England as a region?

2. Do you know of any outstanding courses or units now being taught either in the elementary or secondary schools of (the state) which are aimed at the same objectives as those stated in question one?

These questions can probably be answered in a page or too. The results and conclusions of the study will be made available to you upon its completion. Professor Howard E. Wilson of Harvard University is the sponsor of the study. A stamped and addressed envelope is enclosed for your answer. May I have your help?

Yours very truly,

Royce H. Knapp

APPENDIX B

STATE DEPARTMENT SUPERVISORS WHO PARTICIPATED IN THE SOCIAL-STUDIES SURVEY

State Department of Education, Hartford, Connecticut
  Paul D. Collier, Director, Bureau of Youth Service.
  W. S. Dakin, Senior Supervisor of Rural Education.

State Department of Education, Augusta, Maine
  Earl Hutchinson, Director of Secondary Education.
  R. J. Libby, State Agent for Rural Education.

State Department of Education, Boston, Massachusetts
  A. Russell Mack, Supervisor of Secondary Education.
  Alice B. Beals, Supervisor of Elementary Education.

State Department of Education, Concord, New Hampshire
  Russell H. Leavitt, High School Agent.
  Phila M. Griffin, Elementary School Agent.

State Department of Education, Providence, Rhode Island
  James M. Rockett, Director of Education.
  Francesca DeS. Cosgrove, Principal, Temple Street School, Providence, Rhode Island; selected by Mr. Rockett to speak on elementary-school social-studies programs in Rhode Island.
  Howard D. Wood, Principal, Hope High School, Providence, Rhode Island; selected by Mr. Rockett to speak on the high-school social-studies programs in Rhode Island.

State Department of Education, Montpelier, Vermont
  Max W. Barrows, High School Supervisor.
  Walter F. True, Principal, Randolph High School, Randolph, Vermont; Chairman of the Committee on Curriculum Revision in the Social Studies for the State of Vermont.

APPENDIX C

SOCIAL-STUDIES LEADERS AND CURRICULUM SPECIALISTS

Richard B. Ballou, Professor of Education, Smith College, Northampton, Massachusetts.

Harry W. Berg, Assistant Professor of History, University of New Hampshire, Durham, New Hampshire.

W. Linwood Chase, Professor of Education, Boston University School of Education, Boston, Massachusetts.

Catherine M. Connor, Dean, Rhode Island College of Education, Providence, Rhode Island.

Fred Couey, Associate Professor of Education, University of Connecticut, Storrs, Connecticut.

Katherine H. Daniels, Director of Elementary Education, Hartford, Connecticut.

Elizabeth Gregory, Department of Geography, Keene Teachers College, Keene, New Hampshire.

William T. Gruhn, Assistant Professor of Education, University of Connecticut, Storrs, Connecticut.

Ernest Jackman, Associate Professor of Education, University of Maine, Orono, Maine.

Tyler Kepner, Director of Social Studies, Brookline, Massachusetts.

Henry W. Littlefield, Principal, High School, Hamden, Connecticut.

Glenn W. Moon, Teacher of History, High School, Stamford, Connecticut.

John E. O'Loughlin, Supervising Principal of Elementary Schools, Somerville, Massachusetts.

Arthur E. Pierce, Superintendent of Schools, Bangor, Maine.

Helen J. Piper, Supervisor of Elementary Schools, Lynn, Massachusetts.

Thomas F. Richardson, High School Teacher, New Haven, Connecticut.

Warren Seyfert, Headmaster, Browne and Nichols School, Cambridge, Massachusetts.

Richard J. Stanley, Hall High School, West Hartford, Connecticut.

Howard E. Wilson, Professor of Education, Harvard University, Cambridge, Massachusetts.

APPENDIX D

SOCIAL-STUDIES TEXTBOOKS WIDELY USED IN NEW ENGLAND SCHOOLS [1]

Part One: Elementary Schools

HISTORY

Barker, E. C., Dodd, W. E., and Webb, W. P. *Our Nation Begins.* Evanston, Ill.: Row, Peterson, 1938.

────── *The Story of Our Nation.* Evanston, Ill.: Row, Peterson, 1937.

Clark, M. G., and Gordy, W. F. *Westward Toward America.* New York: Charles Scribner's Sons, 1936.

────── *The First Three Hundred Years in America.* New York: Charles Scribner's Sons, 1934.

Freeland, G. E., Walker, E. E., and Williams, H. E. *America's Building: The Makers of Our Flag.* New York: Charles Scribner's Sons, 1937.

Kelty, Mary G. *The Beginnings of the American People and Nation.* Boston: Ginn and Company, 1937.

────── *The Growth of the American People and Nation.* Boston: Ginn and Company, 1937.

────── *The Story of the American People and Nation.* Boston: Ginn and Company, 1937. A condensation of the two preceding books.

McGuire, Edna. *A Brave Young Land.* New York: The Macmillan Company, 1937.

────── *A Full-Grown Nation.* New York: The Macmillan Company, 1937.

Southworth, J. V., and Southworth, G. V. *The Thirteen American Colonies.* Syracuse, N. Y.: Iroquois Publishing Company, 1935.

[1] Throughout this bibliography of social-studies textbooks only those that deal with the United States are included. Other books which deal with foreign nations and with American backgrounds are widely used, but none of these deals with New England life.

────── *Early Days in America.* Syracuse, N. Y.: Iroquois Publishing Company, 1936.

Woodburn, J. A., and Hill, H. C. *Early America: A History of the United States to 1789.* New York: Longmans, Green and Company, 1934.

GEOGRAPHY

Atwood, W. A., and Thomas, H. G. *The Americas.* Boston: Ginn and Company, 1938.

────── *The Earth and Its People; Lower Book.* Boston: Ginn and Company, 1935.

Barrows, H. H., and Parker, E. P. *United States and Canada.* New York: Silver, Burdett and Company, 1936.

McConnell, W. R. *Living in the Americas.* Chicago: Rand McNally and Company, 1934.

Stull, DeForest, and Hatch, R. W. *Journeys through North America.* New York: Allyn and Bacon, 1938.

CIVICS AND FUSION

Nida, W. L., Campbell, E. F., and Webb, V. L. *The New World Past and Present.* Chicago: Scott, Foresman and Company, 1938.

Rugg, H. O., and Krueger, L. *The Building of America.* Boston: Ginn and Company, 1936.

Wilson, H. E., Wilson, F. H., and Erb, B. P. *Living in the Age of Machines.* New York: American Book Company, 1937.

────── *Richer Ways of Living.* New York: American Book Company, 1937.

Part Two: Junior High School

AMERICAN HISTORY

Casner, M. B., and Gabriel, R. H. *The Rise of American Democracy.* New York: Harcourt, Brace and Company, 1938.

────── *Exploring American History.* New York: Harcourt, Brace and Company, 1935.

Freeland, G. E., and Adams, J. T. *America's Progress in Civilization.* New York: Charles Scribner's Sons, 1938.

Hughes, R. O. *The Making of Our United States.* New York: Allyn and Bacon, 1935.

Moon, Glenn W. *Story of Our Land and People.* New York: Henry Holt and Company, 1938.

Nichols, R. F., Bagley, W. C., and Beard, C. A. *America Yesterday and Today.* New York: The Macmillan Company, 1938. Also available in two parts: Part I, *America Today*; Part II, *America Yesterday.* Same publishing date and company.

Rugg, Harold O. *The Conquest of America: A History of American Civilization, Economic and Social.* Boston: Ginn and Company, 1937.

——— *America's March Toward Democracy; History of American Life, Political and Social.* Boston: Ginn and Company, 1937.

Tryon, R. M., Lingley, C. R., and Morehouse, F. *The American People and Nation.* Boston: Ginn and Company, 1938.

——— *The American Nation; Yesterday and Today.* Boston: Ginn and Company, 1938.

West, W. M., and West, R. *The Story of Our Country.* New York: Allyn and Bacon, 1936.

Woodburn, J. A., Moran, T. F., and Hill, H. C. *Our United States; a History of the Nation.* New York: Longmans, Green and Company, 1938.

GEOGRAPHY

Atwood, W. W., and Thomas, H. G. *The Growth of Nations.* Boston: Ginn and Company, 1936.

——— *The United States among the Nations.* Boston: Ginn and Company, 1934.

McConnell, W. R. *The United States in the Modern World.* New York: Rand McNally and Company, 1939.

Stull, DeForest, and Hatch, R. W. *Our World Today; Asia, Latin America, United States.* New York: Allyn and Bacon, 1938.

CIVICS

Arnold, J. I. *Cooperative Citizenship.* Evanston, Ill.: Row, Peterson, 1933.

Bacon, F. L., and Krug, E. A. *Our Life Today: An Introduction to Current Problems.* Boston: Little, Brown and Company, 1939.

Hill, H. C. *Community and Vocational Civics.* Boston: Ginn and Company, 1936.

——— *Community Civics.* Boston: Ginn and Company, 1928.

Hughes, R. O. *Building Citizenship.* New York: Allyn and Bacon, 1938.

O'Rourke, L. J. *You and Your Community.* Boston: D. C. Heath and Company, 1938.
Young, J. S., and Barton, E. M. *Growing in Citizenship.* New York: McGraw-Hill Book Company, 1939.

FUSION

Rugg, Harold O. *Our Country and Our People.* Boston: Ginn and Company, 1938.

Part Three: Senior High School

AMERICAN HISTORY

Adams, J. T., and Vannest, C. G. *The Record of America.* New York: Charles Scribner's Sons, 1938.
Beard, C. A., and Beard, M. R. *The Making of American Civilization.* New York: The MacMillan Company, 1937.
Faulkner, H. U., and Kepner, Tyler. *America; Its History and People.* New York: Harper and Brothers, 1941.
Hamm, W. A. *The American People: Their History and Their Problems.* Boston: D. C. Heath and Company, 1938.
Muzzey, D. S. *A History of Our Country: A Textbook for High School Students.* Boston: Ginn and Company, 1937.
Wirth, Fremont P. *The Development of America.* New York: American Book Company, 1938.

GEOGRAPHY

Packard, L. O., Sinnott, C. P., and Overton, Bruce. *The Nations at Work: An Industrial and Commercial Geography.* New York: 1939.
Staples, Z. C., and York, G. M. *Economic Geography.* Cincinnati: South-Western Publishing Company, 1934.

ECONOMICS

Carver, T. N., and Carmichael, Maud. *Elementary Economics.* Boston: Ginn and Company, 1937.
Fairchild, F. R. *Economics.* New York: American Book Company, 1938.
Goodman, K. E., and Moore, W. L. *Economics in Everyday Life.* Boston: Ginn and Company, 1938.
Hughes, R. O. *Fundamentals of Economics.* New York: Allyn and Bacon, 1937.

Lutz, H. L., Foote, E. W., and Stanton, B. F. *A New Introduction to Economics.* Evanston, Ill.: Row, Peterson, 1933.

Shields, H. G., and Wilson, W. H. *Business-Economic Problems.* Cincinnati: South-Western Publishing Company, 1935.

SOCIOLOGY

Bogardus, E. S., and Lewis, R. H. *Social Life and Personality.* New York: Silver, Burdett and Company, 1938.

Ellwood, C. A. *Social Problems and Sociology.* New York: American Book Company, 1935.

Gavian, R. W., Gray, A. A., and Groves, E. R. *Our Changing Society: An Introduction to Sociology.* Boston: D. C. Heath and Company, 1939.

Landis, P. H., and Landis, J. T. *Social Living; Principles and Problems in Introductory Sociology.* Boston: Ginn and Company, 1938.

GOVERNMENT

Garner, J. W., and Capen, L. I. *Our Government: Its Nature, Structure, and Functions.* New York: American Book Company, 1938.

Guitteau, W. B., and Bohlman, E. M. *Our Government Today.* Boston: Houghton Mifflin Company, 1938.

Houghton, N. D. *Realities of American Government.* New York: The Macmillan Company, 1937.

Keohane, R. E., Keohane, M. P., and McGoldrick, J. D. *Government in Action: A Study of Problems in American Democracy.* New York: Harcourt, Brace and Company, 1937.

Magruder, Frank A. *American Government.* New York: Allyn and Bacon, 1936.

PROBLEMS OF DEMOCRACY

Greenan, J. T., and Meredith, A. R. *Everyday Problems of American Democracy.* Boston: Houghton Mifflin Company, 1938.

Hughes, R. O. *Problems of American Democracy.* New York: Allyn and Bacon, 1938.

Kidger, H. T. *Problems of American Democracy.* Boston: Ginn and Company, 1940.

Patterson, S. H., Little, A. W. S., and Burch, H. R. *Problems in American Democracy.* New York: The Macmillan Company, 1938.

APPENDIX E

RESOURCES AND TEACHING AIDS FOR TEACHING THE
LIFE AND PROBLEMS OF NEW ENGLAND

Books

ELEMENTARY SCHOOL READING (FICTION)

Curtis, Alice T. *A Little Maid of Massachusetts Colony.* Philadelphia: Penn Publishing Company, 1922.

────── *A Little Maid of Narragansett Bay.* Philadelphia: Penn Publishing Company, 1923.

────── *A Little Maid of Old Connecticut.* Philadelphia: Penn Publishing Company, 1923.

────── *A Little Maid of Ticonderoga.* Philadelphia: Penn Publishing Company, 1899.

Dawes, S. E. *Colonial Massachusetts.* Boston: Silver, Burdett and Company, 1899.

Forbes, H. C. *Applepie Hill.* New York: The Macmillan Company, 1930.

────── *Araminta.* New York: The Macmillan Company, 1927.

Hayes, M. *Little House on Wheels.* Boston: Little, Brown and Company, 1934.

Hill, M. B. *Down-along Apple Market Street.* New York: Frederick A Stokes, 1934.

────── *Summer Comes to Apple Market Street.* New York: Frederick A. Stokes, 1937.

Otis, James. *Mary of Plymouth.* New York: American Book Company, 1910.

Thompson, D. P. *Green Mountain Boys.* Boston: Lothrop, Lee and Shepard, no date.

Wriston, H. T. *Downstreet with Edith.* New York: Doubleday, Doran and Company, 1935.

JUNIOR HIGH SCHOOL READING (FICTION)

Coryell, H. V. *Indian Brother.* New York: Harcourt, Brace and Company, 1935.

Flagg, Mildred B. *Plymouth Maid.* New York: Thomas Nelson and Sons, 1936.

Fox, G. M. *Susan of the Green Mountains*. Boston: Little, Brown and Company, 1937.

Kelly, E. P. *Three Sides of Agiochook*. New York: D. Appleton-Century Company, 1935.

Keyes, M. W. *Juniper Green*. New York: Longmans, Green and Company, 1929.

Lamprey, L. *Tomahawk Trail*. New York: Frederick A. Stokes, 1934.

Updegraff, F. M. *Coat for a Soldier*. New York: Harcourt, Brace and Company, 1941.

Wiggin, K. D. *Rebecca of Sunnybrook Farm*. Boston: Houghton Mifflin Company, 1903.

SENIOR HIGH SCHOOL READING (FICTION)

Allee, M. H. *Jane's Island*. Boston: Houghton, Mifflin Company, 1931.

Bacheller, I. A. *Candle in the Wilderness*. New York: Grosset and Dunlap, 1935.

Freeman, M. E. W. *Humble Romance and Other Stories*. New York: Harper and Brothers, no date.

Larcom, Lucy A. *New England Girlhood*. Boston: Houghton Mifflin and Company, 1899.

Parton, E. *Melissa Ann*. New York: Doubleday, Doran and Company, 1931.

—————— *Runaway Prentice*. New York: Viking Press, 1938.

Wharton, E. *Ethan Frome*. New York: Charles Scribner's Sons, 1938.

Williamson, T. R. *Lobster War*. Boston: Lothrop, Lee and Shepard, 1935.

Wright, P. H. *So We'll Live*. Boston: Houghton Mifflin Company, 1937.

JUNIOR HIGH SCHOOL READING (NONFICTION)

Adams, James T. *Rhode Island's Part in Making America*. Providence: Rhode Island Department of Public Instruction, 1923.

Blough, G. L., McClure, C. H., and Colvin, W. *Fundamentals of Citizenship*. Chicago: Laidlaw Brothers, 1940. (Contains a 94-page supplement on New England.)

APPENDICES

Egan, J. B., and Patton, L. M. *Citizenship in Boston.* Philadelphia: John C. Winston Company, 1925.

Emerson, Philip. *New England Supplement.* New York: The Macmillan Company, 1931. (Geography textbook.)

Finch, Grant E. *New England.* New York: Rand McNally and Company, 1933. (Geography textbook.)

Johnson, C. *New England.* New York: The Macmillan Company, 1929.

Mills, Lewis S. *The Story of Connecticut.* New York: Charles Scribner's Sons, 1926.

Slocum, Harold W. *The Story of Vermont.* New York: Charles Scribner's Sons, 1926.

Winship, A. E. *Great American Educators.* New York: Werner School Book Company, 1900. (Mostly New England educators.)

SENIOR HIGH SCHOOL READING (NONFICTION)

Connolly, J. B. *Out of Gloucester.* New York: Charles Scribner's Sons, 1902.

Early, E. *And This is Cape Cod!* Boston: Houghton Mifflin Company, 1936.

Easton, E. I. *Roger Williams.* Boston: Houghton Mifflin Company, 1930.

Mitchell, E. V. *Maine Summer.* New York: Coward-McCann, 1939.

Robinson, M. L. *Bright Island.* New York: Random House, 1937.

Verrill, A. H. *Heart of Old New England.* New York: Dodd, Mead and Company, 1936.

Selected Maps

Branom, M. E. *Geography Problem Projects: New England States.* Chicago: A. J. Nystrom Company, 1934. (Map problems on physical geography for intermediate grades.)

Massachusetts, Connecticut, Rhode Island: Physical-Political Map. 64 inches by 44 inches. Rand McNally, Chicago.

Maine: Physical-Political Map. 40 inches by 62 inches. Chicago: Rand McNally.

New England — Physical, Political, Industrial Map. 44 inches by 58 inches. Chicago: Denoyer-Geppert.

New Hampshire: Physical-Political Map. 32 inches by 44 inches. Chicago: A. J. Nystrom.

New Hampshire and Vermont: Physical-Political Map. 40 inches by 58 inches. Rand McNally, Chicago.

Selected Films

Early Settlers of New England. (11 minutes, 16-mm, sound.) All grades, Erpi Classroom Films, Inc., 1841 Broadway, New York, N. Y. Shows the hardships of colonial life, the social life of a colonial community, and emphasizes the role of religion upon life in early New England. Indicates the motives of the colonists for coming to the New England region.

Colonial Children. (11 minutes, 16-mm, sound.) Primary, Intermediate, and Junior High. Erpi Classroom Films, Inc., 1841 Broadway, New York, N. Y. Shows dress, household equipment, manners, and family life in late 17th-century New England. A day of life in a New England colonial home.

Shell Fishing. (11 minutes, 16-mm, sound.) All grades. Erpi Classroom Films, Inc., 1841 Broadway, New York, N. Y. Catching, canning, packing, and marketing of clams, oysters, crabs, and lobsters. Conservation problems are emphasized. Deals largely with New England coasts.

New England Fisheries. (24 minutes, 16-mm, silent.) Part I, "Cod," 16 minutes; Part II, "Mackerel," 8 minutes. All grades. Eastman Kodak Company, Rochester, New York. Shows trawling for cod and seining for mackerel and fish preparation at Gloucester. Shows how fishing boats and ships are built. Map shows location of Grand Banks.

New England Fisherman. (11 minutes, 16-mm, sound.) All grades. Erpi Classroom Films, Inc., 1841 Broadway, New York, N. Y. The ways of living and the social life of the fishermen of New England are shown. Contrasts old and modern methods of fishing.

Selected Periodicals Dealing with New England

New England Councilor. The bulletins of the New England Council for the Social Studies. Mimeographed. Published Monthly. School of Education, Boston University, Boston, Massachusetts. The *Councilor* reports on activities in the social studies in New

England. It suggests materials and ideas for the improvement of social studies in New England schools.

New England Newsletter. Published monthly by the New England Council, Statler Building, Boston, Massachusetts. The *Newsletter* is the organ of the New England Council, and has as its objective the reporting of industrial trends, opportunities, and economic problems of New England business.

New England Planning Bulletin. Published occasionally by the New England Regional Planning Commission, Federal Building, Boston, Massachusetts. The Bulletin deals with problems of local and regional planning in New England. It presents new viewpoints, indicates problems, and suggests solutions to local and regional problems.

New England Quarterly. Published quarterly. New England Quarterly, 200 Stephens Hall, Orono, Maine. The *Quarterly* carries scholarly articles on the history, literature, and philosophy of New England.

Yankee. Published monthly at Dublin, New Hampshire. The *Yankee* is an informal magazine that deals with local color, traditions, and life of New England.

和
BIBLIOGRAPHY

BIBLIOGRAPHY

BOOKS

Adams, James T. *The Founding of New England.* Boston: Atlantic Monthly Press, 1922.

———*Revolutionary New England.* Boston: Atlantic Monthly Press, 1924.

———*New England in the Republic.* Boston: Little, Brown & Co., 1926.

Ackerman, Edward A. *New England's Fishing Industry.* Chicago: The University of Chicago Press, 1941.

Baker, O. E. (ed.). *Atlas of American Agriculture.* Washington, D.C.: U. S. Department of Agriculture, 1936.

Bernard, L. L. (ed.). *The Fields and Methods of Sociology.* New York: Farrar and Rinehart, 1934.

Boaz, Franz. *Anthropology and Modern Life.* New York: W. W. Norton & Co., 1928.

Borg, C. O. *The Great Southwest.* Santa Ana, California: Fine Arts Press, 1936.

Bowman, Isaiah. *Forest Physiography.* New York: John Wiley & Sons, 1911.

———*Geography in Relation to the Social Sciences.* New York: Charles Scribner's Sons, 1934.

Branford, Victor. *The Regional Survey as a Method of Social Study.* Oxford: Holywell Press, 1915.

———and Geddes, Patrick. *Our Social Inheritance.* London: Williams and Norgate, 1919.

Brigham, Albert P. *Geographic Influences in American History.* New York: Ginn and Company, 1903.

Brooks, Van Wyck. *The Flowering of New England.* New York: E. P. Dutton & Co., 1936.

———*New England: Indian Summer.* New York: E. P. Dutton & Co., 1940.

Brunhes, Jean, *Human Geography.* New York: Rand McNally & Co., 1920. (Translated by Isaiah Bowman and Ellwood Dodd.)

Brewer, Daniel C. *The Conquest of New England by the Immigrant.* New York: G. P. Putnam's Sons, 1926.

Burgess, Ernest W. (ed.). *The Urban Community.* Chicago: University of Chicago Press, 1926.

———— and Blumer, H. (ed.). *Human Side of Social Planning.* Chicago: American Sociological Society, 1936.

Campbell, J. C. *The Southern Highlander and His Home Land.* New York: Russell Sage Foundation, 1921.

Colby, C. C. *Source Book for the Economic Geography of North America.* Chicago: University of Chicago Press, 1916.

Cole, W. E., and Crowe, H. P. *Recent Trends in Rural Planning.* New York: Prentice-Hall, 1937.

Dame, Lawrence. *New England Comes Back.* New York: Random House, 1940.

Daniels, Jonathan. *A Southerner Discovers New England.* New York: The Macmillan Company, 1940.

Davidson, Donald. *The Attack on Leviathan: Regionalism and Nationalism in the United States.* Chapel Hill: The University of North Carolina Press, 1938.

Davis, W. T. *The New England States: Their Constitutional, Judicial, Educational, Commercial, Professional, and Industrial History.* 4 volumes. Boston: D. H. Hurd Company, 1897.

Dickinson, R. E., and Howarth, O. J. R. *The Making of Geography.* Oxford: Clarendon Press, 1933.

Dixon, R. B. *The Building of Cultures.* New York: Charles Scribner's Sons, 1928.

Duffus, R. L. *Mastering a Metropolis: Planning the Future of the New York Regions.* New York: Harper & Brothers, 1930.

Early, Eleanor. *A New England Sampler.* Boston: Waverly House, 1940.

Elliott, F. F. *Types of Farming in the United States.* Washington, D.C.: U. S. Government Printing Office, 1933.

Elliott, W. Y. *The Need for Constitutional Reform.* New York: McGraw-Hill Book Company, 1935.

Engeln, O. D. *Inheriting the Earth, or the Geographical Factor in National Development.* New York: The Macmillan Company, 1922.

Fagg, C. C., and Hutchings, G. E. *An Introduction to Regional Surveying.* Cambridge: University Press, 1930.

Federal Writers' Project of the Works Progress Administration for the State of Maine. *Maine: A Guide "Down East."* Boston: Houghton Mifflin, 1937.

Federal Writers' Project of the Works Progress Administration for the State of Massachusetts. *Massachusetts: A Guide to Its Places and People.* Boston: Houghton Mifflin, 1937.

Federal Writers' Project of the Works Progress Administration for the State of Vermont. *Vermont: A Guide to the Green Mountain State.* Boston: Houghton Mifflin, 1937.

Federal Writers' Project of the Works Progress Administration for the State of Rhode Island. *Rhode Island: A Guide to the Smallest State.* Boston: Houghton Mifflin, 1937.

Federal Writers' Project of the Works Progress Administration for the State of Connecticut. *Connecticut: A Guide to Its Roads, Lore, and People.* Boston: Houghton Mifflin, 1937.

Federal Writers' Project of the Works Progress Administration for the State of New Hampshire. *New Hampshire: A Guide to the Granite State.* Boston: Houghton Mifflin, 1937.

Federal Writers' Project of the Works Progress Administration. *Here's New England.* Boston: Houghton Mifflin, 1937.

Fenneman, N. M. *Physiography of Western United States.* New York: McGraw-Hill Book Company, 1931.

Finch, V. C., and Baker, O. E. *Geography of the World's Agriculture.* Washington, D.C.: U. S. Department of Agriculture, 1911.

Finch, V. C., and Trewartha, G. T. *Elements of Geography.* New York: McGraw-Hill Book Company, 1937.

Fleure, H. J. *The Geographical Background of Modern Problems.* New York: Longmans, Green & Co., 1932.

Foreign Commerce Yearbook. Washington, D.C.: U. S. Department of Commerce, 1938.

Fiske, John, *The Beginnings of New England.* Boston: Houghton Mifflin, 1889.

Gooch, R. K. *Regionalism in France.* (University of Virginia, Institute for Research in the Social Sciences, Bulletin No. 12.) New York: The Century Company, 1931.

Gould, J. *New England Town Meeting.* Brattleboro, Vt.: Stephen Daye Press, 1940.

Hacker, L. M., and Kendrick, B. B. *The United States Since 1865.* New York: F. S. Crofts & Co., 1932.

Hahn, Aubrey. "The Role of the Community School in Educating for the Use of the Natural and Human Resources in the Pacific Northwest." Unpublished Doctoral Dissertation, Stanford University, 1940.

Hartford, Ellis F. "Educational Policy for Regional Well-Being in the Southeast." Unpublished Doctoral Dissertation, Harvard University, 1941.

Holmes, Henry W. *The Road to Courage.* New York: Alfred A. Knopf, 1943.

Kolb, J. H., and Brunner, E. de S. *A Study of Rural Society.* Boston: Houghton Mifflin, 1935.

Krey, A. C. *A Regional Program for the Social Studies.* New York: The Macmillan Company, 1938.

Laughlin, C. E. *So You're Seeing New England.* Boston: Little, Brown & Co., 1940.

Linton, Ralph. *The Study of Man.* New York: D. Appleton–Century Co., 1929.

Logasa, Hannah. *Regional United States: A Subject List.* Boston: F. W. Faxon Company, 1942.

Lynd, R. S., and Lynd, H. M. *Middletown.* New York: Harcourt, Brace and Co., 1929.

McKenzie, R. D. *The Metropolitan Community.* New York: McGraw-Hill Book Company, 1932.

McWilliams, Carey. *The New Regionalism in American Literature.* Seattle: University of Washington Book Store, 1930.

Moore, Harry E. *What is Regionalism?* Chapel Hill: The University of North Carolina Press, 1937.

Mukerjee, Radhakamal. *Regional Sociology.* New York: The Century Co., 1926.

Mumford, Lewis. *The Culture of Cities.* New York: Harcourt, Brace and Co., 1938.

Merriam, C. E., and Gosnell, H. F. *The American Party System.* New York: The Macmillan Company, 1940.

BIBLIOGRAPHY 147

Odum, Howard W. *An American Epoch.* New York: Henry Holt & Company. 1930.

——— and Moore, Harry E. *American Regionalism.* New York: Henry Holt & Company, 1938.

——— *The Regional Approach to National Social Planning.* New York: Foreign Policy Association, and Chapel Hill: The University of North Carolina Press, 1935.

——— *Southern Regions of the United States.* Chapel Hill: The University of North Carolina Press, 1936.

Ogburn, W. F., and Goldenweiser, A. *The Social Sciences and Their Interrelations.* Boston: Houghton Mifflin, 1927.

President's Research Committee on Social Trends, *Recent Social Trends,* 2 volumes. New York: McGraw-Hill Book Company, 1933.

Ratzel, Friedrich. *Anthropogeographie.* Stuttgart: J. Engelhorn, 1921.

Semple, Ellen C. *American History and Its Geographic Influences.* Boston: Houghton Mifflin, 1903.

Smith, J. R. *North America: Its Peoples and Resources, Development, and Prospects as an Agricultural, Industrial, and Commercial Area.* New York: Harcourt, Brace & Co., 1925.

Thomas, Franklin. *The Environmental Basis of Society.* New York: The Century Co., 1925.

Turner, F. J. *The Significance of Sections in American History.* New York: Henry Holt and Company, 1932.

Ulich, Robert. *Fundamentals of Democratic Education.* New York: The American Book Company, 1940.

Vance, R. B. *Human Geography of the South.* Chapel Hill: The University of North Carolina Press, 1932.

Verrill, A. H. *Along New England Shores.* New York: G. P. Putnam's Sons, 1936.

——— *Heart of Old New England.* New York: Dodd, Mead & Co., 1936.

Vidal de la Blache, P. M. J. *Principles of Human Geography.* Edited by E. de Martonne; translated by Millicent T. Bingham. New York: Henry Holt & Company, 1926.

Webb, W. P. *The Great Plains.* Boston: Ginn and Co., 1931.

Weeden, W. B. *Economic and Social History of New England.* 2 volumes. Boston: Houghton Mifflin, 1891.

Wesley, Edgar B. *Teaching the Social Studies.* 2nd Edition. Boston: D. C. Heath & Co., 1942.

White, C. L., and Renner, G. T. *Geography: An Introduction to Human Ecology.* New York: The Century Company, 1936.

Wilson, Howard E. *Education for Citizenship.* New York: McGraw-Hill Book Company, 1938.

Wissler, Clark. *The American Indian.* 3rd edition. New York: Oxford University Press, 1938.

Wolfanger, L. A. *The Major Soil Divisions of the United States.* New York: John Wiley and Sons, 1930.

Wright, F. W. (editor). *New England's Prospect.* New York: American Geographical Society, 1933.

Zimmerman, E. W. *World Resources and Industries.* New York: Harper and Brothers, 1933.

PAMPHLETS, MONOGRAPHS, AND BULLETINS

Connecticut State Planning Board. *Summary of the Work of the Connecticut State Planning Board.* Public Document No. 87. Hartford: Connecticut State Planning Board, 1937.

Connecticut State Agricultural Experiment Station. *Better Forests for Connecticut.* Bulletin No. 253. New Haven: Agricultural Experiment Station, 1924.

Maine Agricultural Experiment Station. *Costs and Returns in Producing Potatoes in Aroostook County, Maine.* Bulletin No. 390. Orono: Experiment Station, 1937.

Maine State Planning Board. *Report: 1934–1935.* Augusta: The Board, 1935.

Massachusetts State Planning Board. *First Report: 1935.* Boston: The Board, 1935.

———— *Progress on State Planning for Massachusetts.* Boston: Massachusetts State Planning Board, 1936.

Massachusetts State Agricultural Experiment Station. *Part-Time Farming in Massachusetts.* Amherst: Experiment Station, 1930.

Murra, Wilbur F., and others. *Bibliography of Textbooks in the Social Studies.* Bulletin No. 12. Cambridge: National Council for the Social Studies, 1939.

National Resources Committee. *Regional Planning, Part III, — New England.* Washington, D.C.: U. S. Government Printing Office, 1936.
——— *Regional Factors in National Planning.* Washington, D.C.: U. S. Government Printing Office, 1935.
New England Regional Planning Commission, Region I of the National Resources Planning Board, Boston, Massachusetts. The following bulletins and monographs:
——— *Economic Conditions of New England.* May, 1939.
——— *From the Ground Up.* March, 1939.
——— *Is Planning Practical for Your Town?* March, 1939.
——— *Permanent Defense of New England.* March, 1941.
——— *Preliminary Statement, Regional Development Plan, New England.* December, 1942.
——— *The Rivers Speak.* January, 1942.
——— *Water Resources of New England.* December, 1937.
New Hampshire State Development Commission, *First Biennial Report.* Concord: The Commission, 1937.
——— *State Planning in New Hampshire.* Concord: The Commission, 1935.
Rhode Island State Planning Board, *Agriculture in Rhode Island.* Providence: The Board, 1937.
——— *Planning and Zoning in Rhode Island.* Providence: The Board, 1937.
——— *Rhode Island Commercial Fisheries.* Providence: The Board, 1936.
——— *Rhode Island Population Trends.* Providence: The Board, 1936.
——— *Rhode Island Water Resources.* Providence: The Board, 1936.
Vermont State Planning Board. *Report of the State Planning Board,* 1937–1938. Montpelier: The Board, 1938.

MAGAZINE ARTICLES

Adams, Charles, "Regional Planning in Relation to Public Administration," *National Municipal Review,* 15:35–42. January 1926.

―――― "Social Objectives of Regional Planning." *National Municipal Review*, 15:79–87. February 1926.

Ascher, C. S. "Regionalism, Charting the Future." *Survey*, 66:460–461. October 1, 1932.

―――― "Regionalism, a New Approach to the Good Life." *National Municipal Review*, 20:592–596. October 1931.

Baker, J. E. "Regionalism in the Middle West." *American Review*, 4:603–614. March 1935.

Baker, O. E. "Agricultural Regions of North America." *Economic Geography*, 2:459–493, October 1926; 3:50–86, January 1927; 3:309–339, July 1927; 4:44–73, January 1928; 4:399–433, October 1928; 5:36–69, January 1939; 6:166–190, April 1930.

Barrows, E. M. "United Regions of America, A New American Nation." *New Outlook*, 161:16–25. May 1933.

Beard, C. A. "Some Aspects of Regional Planning." *American Political Science Review*, 20:273–283. May 1926.

Botkin, B. A. "Regionalism: Cult or Culture?" *English Journal*, 25:181–185. March 1936.

Brown, E. F. "The Tennessee Valley Idea." *Current History*, 40:410–417. July 1934.

Burgess, E. W. "The New Community and Its Future." *Annals of the American Academy of Political and Social Science*, 149:157–164. May 1930.

Calrow, C. J. "Interstate Cooperation." *National Municipal Review*, 25:445–451. August 1936.

Davidson, Donald. "The Political Economy of Regionalism." *American Review*, 6:410–434. February 1936.

―――― "Where Regionalism and Sectionalism Meet." *Social Forces*, 13:176–183. October 1934.

Dewey, John. "Americanism and Localism." *Dial*, 68:684–688. June 1920.

Dryer, C. R. "Natural Economic Regions." *Annals of the Association of American Geographers*, 5:121–125. 1915.

Eliot, C. W. "National Planning." *City Planning*, 10:103–111. July 1934.

Fenneman, N. M. "Physiographic Boundaries within the United States." *Annals of the Association of American Geographers*, 4:84–134. 1914.
────── "Physiographic Divisions of the United States." *Annals of the Association of American Geographers*, 18:261–353. December 1928.
Fesler, J. W. "Federal Administrative Regions." *American Political Science Review*, 30:257–268. April 1936.
────── "Standardization of Federal Administrative Regions." *Social Forces*, 15:12–21. October 1936.
Fletcher, J. G. "Regionalism and Folk Art." *Southwest Review*, 19:429–434. July 1934.
Fleure, H. J. "Human Regions." *Scottish Geographical Magazine*, 35:94–105. March 1919.
Fohmann, K. B. "Helping Our Youth to Think in Terms of Regions." *City Planning*, 9:168–171. October 1933.
Frankfurter, Felix, and Landis, J. M. "The Compact Clause of the Constitution — A Study in Interstate Adjustments." *Yale Law Journal*, 34:685–758. May 1925.
Geddes, Patrick. "Mapping of Life." *Sociological Review*, 16:193–203. July 1924.
Goldenweiser, A. A. "Culture and Environment." *American Journal of Sociology*, 21:628–633. March 1916.
Gras, N. S. B. "Development of Metropolitan Economy in Europe and America." *American Historical Review*, 27:695–708. July 1922.
────── "Regionalism and Nationalism." *Foreign Affairs*, 7:454–467. April 1929.
Hayes, Z. M. "Bibliography of Regional Planning." *Bulletin of Bibliography*, 13:65–69. September 1927.
Hintze, Hedwig. "Regionalism." *Encyclopaedia of the Social Sciences*, 13:208–218.
Holmes, W. H. "Areas of American Culture, Characterization as an Aid in the Study of the Antiquities." *American Anthropologist*, New Series, 16:413–446. July 1914.
Hypes, J. L. "Geography, A Social Determinant." *Journal of Rural Education*, 4:193–204. January 1925.

Ickes, H. L. "Saving the Good Earth; The Mississippi Valley Committee and Its Plan." *Survey Graphic*, 23:52–59. February 1934.

Jefferson, Mark. "Some Considerations on the Geographical Provinces of the United States." *Annals of the Association of American Geographers*, 7:3–15. 1917.

Joerg, W. L. G. "The Subdivisions of North America into Natural Regions, A Preliminary Inquiry." *Annals of the Association of American Geographers*, 4:55–83. 1914.

Knapp, R. H. "American Regionalism and Social Education." *Social Education*, 6:361–363. December 1942.

Lewis, B. G. "Regionalism, A Plan for Uniting the States More Effectively." *The Forum*, 89:136–141. March 1933.

Mackaye, Benton. "Regional Planning." *Sociological Review*, 20: 293–299. October 1928.

Mackmurdo, A. H. "Regional Social Unit." *Sociological Review*, 24:14–23. January 1932.

McKenzie, R. D. "The Ecological Approach to the Study of the Human Community." *American Journal of Sociology*, 30: 287–301. November 1924.

Merriam, C. E. "Planning Agencies in America." *American Political Science Review*, 29:197–211. April 1935.

Mukerjee, Radhakamal. "The Processes of Regional Balance." *Sociological Review*, 23:173–181. October 1931.

——— "Regional Balance of Man." *American Journal of Sociology*, 36:455–460. November 1930.

Mumford, Lewis. "Regionalism and Irregionalism." *Sociological Review*, 19:277–288, October 1927; 20: 18–33, 131–141, April 1928.

——— "Regions — To Live In." *Survey Graphic*, 54:151–152. May 1925.

——— "Relation of Nationalism and Culture." *Sociological Review*, 14:315–319. October 1922.

——— "Social Responsibilities of Teachers and Their Implications for Teacher Education." *Educational Record*, 20:471–499. October 1939.

——— "The Theory and Practice of Regionalism." *Sociological Review*, 20:18–33, 131–141. January-April 1928.

Odum, Howard W. "The Case for Regional National Social Planning." *Social Forces*, 13:6–23. October 1934.
——— "Notes on the Study of Regional and Folk Society." *Social Forces*, 10:164–175. December 1931.
——— "Regionalism Versus Sectionalism in the South's Place in the National Economy." *Social Forces*, 12:338–346. March 1934.
——— "Realistic Premises for Regional Planning Objectives." *Plan Age*, 2:7–23. March 1936.
Ogburn, W. F. "Regions." *Social Forces*, 15:6–11. October 1936.
Park, R. E. "Social Planning and Human Nature." *Publication of the American Sociological Society*, 29:19–28. August 1935.
——— "Succession, an Ecological Concept." *American Sociological Review*, 1:171–179. April 1936.
Parsons, P. A. "Passing of Sectionalism." *New Republic*, 27:60–63. June 1921.
Ransom, J. C. "The Aesthetics of Regionalism." *American Review*, 2:290–310. January 1934.
Renner, G. T. "The Statistical Approach to Regions." *Annals of the Association of American Geographers*, 25:137–145. September 1935.
——— "The Nature of Geographical Ideas." *Teachers College Record*, 43:597–610. May 1942.
——— and Renner, M. P. "Regionalism in American Life." *Teachers College Record*, 43:337–357. February 1942.
Roosevelt, F. D. "Growing Up by Plan." *Survey Graphic*, 67:483–485. February 1932.
Sauer, C. O. "Cultural Geography." *Encyclopaedia of the Social Sciences*, 6:621–624.
——— "The Survey Method in Geography and Its Objectives." *Annals of the Association of American Geographers*, 14:17–33. March 1924.
Strong, H. M. "Regionalism, Its Cultural Significance." *Economic Geography*, 12:392–412. October 1936.
"A Symposium on Regional Planning." *Survey Graphic, Regionalism Number*. May 1925.
Tate, Allen. "Regionalism and Sectionalism." *New Republic*, 59:158–161. December 1931.

Turner, F. J. "Geographic Influences in American Political History." *Bulletin of the American Geographic Society*, 46:591–595. August 1914.

────── "Geographic Sectionalism in American History." *Annals of the Association of American Geographers*. 16:85–93. June 1926.

────── "Sectionalism in America." *American Journal of Sociology*, 13:661–675. May 1908.

"Twelve Planning Regions Established." *American City*, 49:81. April 1934.

Vance, R. B. "Concept of the Region." *Social Forces*, 8:202–218. December 1929.

────── "Implications of the Concept 'Region and Regional Planning'." *Publications of the American Sociological Society*, 29:85–93. August 1935.

Van Cleef, E. "Philosophy and Geography and Geographical Regions." *Geographical Review*, 22:497–498. July 1932.

Whitaker, J. R. "Regional Interdependence." *Journal of Geography*, 31:164–165. April 1932.

Whitbeck, R. H. "Facts and Fiction in Geography by Natural Regions." *Journal of Geography*, 22:86–94. March 1923.

Wirth, Louis. "Localism, Regionalism, and Centralization." *The American Journal of Sociology*, 42:493–509. January 1937.

────── "The Prospects of Regional Research in Relation to Social Planning." *Publications of the American Sociological Society*, 29:107–114. August 1935.

INDEX

Adams, J. T., 48
Aesthetic regionalism, 33
Agricultural regions, 23
American regionalism, implications for social education, 6–7; implications for social studies, 37–40
Anthropology and regionalism, 28

Brunhes, 14
Bryant, William Cullen, 34

Cance, A. E., 66
Chase, Mary Ellen, 35
Cogswell, E. C., 64
Columbia University, 8
Commercial regions, 21
Commercial geography, 20
Communication systems, 21
Connecticut Agricultural College, 54
Culture area, 28
Culture patterns, 21

Davis, I. G., 54
Dickinson, R. E., 14

Economic geographers, 20
Economic imbalance, 22
Economics and regionalism, 20
Economic regionalist, 22
Economic regions, 21
Education and national welfare, 122
Educational policy and regional well-being, 39
Elliott, W. Y., 27

Federalism, 24
Federal regions, 27
Federal Reserve System, 22
Fenneman, N. M., 17
Ferber, Edna, 35
Finch, J. C., 16
Fisher, R. T., 45

Geographical studies, nature of, 15
Geographic regions, 19

Geography, environmentalists, 15; possibilists, 15; regional idea, 20
Gosnell, H. F., 25
Greeley, W. R., 41

Hahn, Aubrey, 7
Hanna, Paul R., 7
Hartford, Ellis F., 8
Harvard Forest, 45
Harvard University, 8
Herbertson, 14
Hingham, Mass., 89
Holmes, Henry Wyman, 5
Howarth, O. J. R., 14
Huckleberry Finn, 34
Hypes, J. L., 66

Innocents Abroad, 34
Irving, Washington, 34

Knapp, R. H., 9
Knickerbocker's History of New York, 34
Krey, A. C., 6

Land-use problem region, 26–27
Last of the Mohicans, The, 34
Leatherstocking Tales, 34
Legend of Sleepy Hollow, The, 34
Limitations of study, 11, 12
Literary regionalism, 33

McKenzie, R. D., 31
Manufactural regions, 23
Manufacturing regions, 21
Marginal lands, 21
Merriam, C. E., 25
Method of the study, 10
Metropolitan regions, 32
Metropolitan regionalism, 31
Minnesota, University of, 6
Mitchell, Margaret, 35
Moore, H. E., 29
Mumford, Lewis, 8, 37

INDEX

National Resources Committee, 26
New England, aesthetic resources, 51; agriculture, 54–55; climate, 43–44; commerce, 58; conservation problems, 60; cultural heritage, 49; economy, 51; elementary schools, 104–106; farming, 55–56; fishing, 46; forests, 45; geographic factors, 42; junior high schools, 106–108; manufactures, 52; mineral resources, 47; physical divisions, 43; political candidates, 50; population, 48; problems, 9; raw materials, 53; recreational resources, 57; regional problems, 59; religious life, 50; rural maladjustment, 64; senior high schools, 108–115; schools teaching regional life and problems, 74–92; social welfare problems, 65; transportation problems, 62–63; trends in regional integration, 66–71; water resources, 46; what the schools ought to teach, 93–103
New England Council for the Social Studies, 87
New England History Teachers' Association, 87
New England Regional Planning Commission, 46
North American Indian, 29
North Carolina, University of, 8

Odum, Howard W., 8, 29

Philosophical setting of the study, 3
Political regionalists, 26
Political science and regionalism, 24
Problem of this study, 9–10
Progressive Education Association, 7
Puritanism, 41

Questionnaire, 85–87

Ratzel, F., 14, 15
Recommendations, for regional cooperation, 121; for teacher training, 120
Regional anthropologists, 30
Regional approach, 5
Regional decentralization, 22
Regional planning, 5, 31

Regional portraiture, 35
Regional sociologists, 30
Regionalism, in American politics, 25; and education, 8; meaning of, 37; rise of, 5; and sectionalism, 36; and social studies, 37
Renner, George T., 8
Resource patterns, 21
Ritter, 14

Sectionalism, 24–25
Semple, Ellen C., 15
Social control, 24
Social planning, sociological approach, 33
Social research, 4
Social sciences, philosophy of regionalism in, 13
Social studies, definition of, 4
Social studies and social sciences, 37
Socio-economic regions, 31, 32
Sociology and regionalism, 30
Solid South, 25
Sources of this study, 10, 11
Stanford University, 7, 8
Steinbeck, John, 35
Submarginal regions, 21
Subregions, 22

Teaching materials on New England, 135–139
Tennessee Valley Authority, 26
Tom Sawyer, 34
Trewartha, G. T., 16
Turner, F. J., 24, 25
Twain, Mark, 34

Ulich, Robert, 3
Urban-rural competition, 30

Vegetation regions, 19

Wilson, Howard E., 8
Wisconsin, University of, 16
Wissler, Clark, 28
Wolfanger, Louis, 18
Wright, J. K., 18

Yale School of Forestry, 45

Zimmerman, E. W., 21